gorillatheatre

gorillatheatre

a practical guide to

performing the new outdoor

theatre anytime, anywhere

Christopher Carter Sanderson

A THEATRE ARTS BOOK   *Routledge*   *New York & London*

A Theatre Arts Book
Published in 2003 by
Routledge
29 West 35th Street
New York, NY 10001
www.routledge-ny.com

Published in Great Britain by
Routledge
11 New Fetter Lane
London EC4P 4EE
www.routledge.co.uk

Copyright © 2003 by Taylor & Francis Books, Inc.
Routledge is an imprint of the Taylor & Francis Group.

Printed in the United States of America on acid-free paper.

10 9 8 7 6 5 4 3 2 1

Library of Congress Cataloging in Publication Data

Sanderson, Christopher Carter, 1965–
    Gorilla theatre : a practical guide to performing the new outdoor theatre anytime, anywhere / Christopher Carter Sanderson.
        p. cm.
Includes bibliographical references and index.
    ISBN 0–87830–170–4 (HB : alk. paper) — ISBN 0–87830–171–2 (PB : alk. paper)
    1. Gorilla Repertory Theatre Company. 2. Acting. 3. Theater—Production and direction. I. Title.
        PN2297.G67S26 2003
        792'.028—dc21   2003001503

For Frances

Scientia sine Arte nihil est; Ars sine Scientia nihil est.

contents

12. Moving a Show   161

Feel of the Show
Moving A Midsummer Night's Dream: *"Get Puck!" and Other Stories*

13. Notes and Observations   167

Dialogue with Criticism
Relationship to Academia
Sibling Institutions

14. Spirituality   175

BIBLIOGRAPHY   181
INDEX   183

foreword

Summers in New York City nowadays burst with theatre. There are nights in July and August when you can walk Central Park end to end (north to south, I mean) and stumble upon four or five different troupes cavorting among the greenery, bringing drama to life for an audience of diehards and passersby. It's probably not too much of an exaggeration to say that all are the direct result of the success of Christopher Sanderson's Gorilla Rep, which transformed guerrilla theatre into gorilla theatre and made outdoor drama not just accessible but excellent.

The variety is enormous, everything from classics by Shakespeare and Molière to contemporary experimental work by the likes of Mac Wellman. What's consistent is the aesthetic; every one of these shows is an instance of gorilla theatre—an opportunity to bring actors and audience together in nature and under the stars, the way the Greeks conceived of drama in the first place, where we share the passion and joy and spectacular heightened emotion that reminds us why the heck theatre is so vital and necessary.

Gorilla theatre means several things, all due to the pioneering influence of Christopher Carter Sanderson. It's free. It's outside. It's high energy. It requires bottled water and comfortable shoes because the audience almost always has to follow the actors around a park from scene to scene on a warm summer night.

Gorilla theatre is, of course, the subject of this book, and few living directors know more about how to do it well than Christopher Carter Sanderson. Anybody with nerve can put on a show in the middle of a park, and they will probably get some attention, at least for a while—

that's busking, and it's cool. But what Sanderson has refined and codified, in this book, is a theatre that moves beyond momentary diversion. Gorilla theatre—as practiced since 1989 by Gorilla Rep, the company Sanderson founded—constantly surprises and engages and astonishes.

Take Gorilla Rep's signature piece, *A Midsummer Night's Dream*, which has been performed in Washington Square Park in New York City every summer since 1989. James Ireland Baker (*Time Out New York*, 1996) said the production "strikes a note of otherworldly awe" because of "audience proximity and the fluid use of the park space"; Ben Brantley (*New York Times*, 1994) noted that "The complicity between actors and audiences is as genial and unforced as theatre allows. And when we finally reach the celebratory play-within-the-play, it feels like an exultant metaphor for everything that's gone before."

Note those words *awe* and *celebratory*: they're spot-on in describing the experience of gorilla theatre when it's done right. Here's how I described Sanderson's eerily magical *Macbeth* in a **nytheater.com** review in 2000:

> Played on the Shakespeare Lawn at Fort Tryon Park, against a backdrop of craggy trees between whose leaves we can spy the splendor of both the Cloisters and the Hudson River, the familiar play comes alive under the remarkable direction of Christopher Carter Sanderson and the vivid and vigorous acting of its sixteen actors. Lighting is provided from above by whatever celestial bodies inhabit the night sky, and from below by Gorilla Rep's trademark mega-watt torches, skillfully operated by Sanderson and various actors doubling as handlers. The resultant grand shadows tower against what feels more and more, as night falls, like dense forest. We are transported to the moody, mysterious Scottish landscape of the play: a place where witches and wickedness feel right at home: a spectacular setting for a ghost story like this one.

And here's my attempt to convey what Sanderson's *Cymbeline* (2001) was like:

> Gorilla Rep's *Cymbeline* is a living tribute to Shakespeare as storyteller: against the odds and our better judgment, we find ourselves utterly caught up in the thing, entranced and enchanted and eager to learn what's going to happen next. It's also a tribute to the artistry of Gorilla Rep's founder Christopher Carter Sanderson, who has staged it in the most gloriously

stage-y natural settings imaginable and paced it within an inch of its life to ensure that no one in earshot is going to be bored and that no one, no matter how slowly he or she trudges from one scene to the next, will miss anything important.

Even on those rare occasions when Sanderson has the audience sit still for two hours, as he did with his mounting of *Othello*, the work is relentlessly involving: I left that production wishing I had never read or seen the play before, because Sanderson's crisp, thoughtful staging crystallized so many of its themes with incisiveness and clarity.

For here is the real essence of the gorilla aesthetic: Sanderson doesn't make his audience run around merrily after his actors just for the fun of it (though that's almost always the result). No, the notion here is to put us inside the drama; to make us active (not interactive) participants in the yarn that's being spun. In a **nytheater.com** interview, Sanderson told me the following:

> We use what I call audience inclusion, not audience participation. The audience is supposed to be part of the performance, but in a detailed, omnipresent way. That's what Shakespeare wrote for. When Shakespeare writes a monologue, you have to ask, who is the character talking to? He's not talking to his toes. He needs the audience. In the first scene of *Midsummer Night's Dream*, the audience is the rest of the court. There are many techniques that can be used to include the audience. When you ignore this, you lock them into one relationship. They are voyeurs. You must respond to the audience like it was another actor.

Sanderson scouts outdoor locations to set his plays amid nature's magisterial grandeur—this reminds us of the sacred mission of theatre, easing us toward catharsis. And then he sets his actors to work with emotion, power, and energy. It looks easy—it's not—but it almost always works. People who resist outdoor theatre (and I number myself among them) are won over by the real electricity Sanderson and his collaborators generate without a single electrical outlet. Gorilla theatre is theatre of urgency and connection.

And lest you think the gorilla paradigm is only good for tried-and-true classics, be aware that several extraordinary new plays have had their genesis in the world of gorilla theatre. Sanderson commissioned works like Chris Barron and Kirk Bromley's *Faust* and Matt Freeman's *The*

Death of King Arthur, which premiered under the auspices of Gorilla Rep, demonstrating conclusively that literate new drama can be developed outside the confines of what critic Neil Genzlinger called "stodgy" indoor theatre. Sanderson himself even adapted a spanking-new naughty *UBU IS KING!*, bringing Alfred Jarry's scatological stunt of a play squarely into the universe of Mayor Giuliani's New York City. Its success derived largely from the brazen audacity of its unorthodox staging, in unexpected style and in unexpected places all over the urban island that Sanderson thinks of as his stage.

I'm a theatre reviewer, mostly, so it's not important that I understand the inner workings of Sanderson's gorilla-theatre concepts. But I rejoice in the fact that he's written down the concepts so that others can learn what he's discovered about how to make outdoor theatre into an enlarging, enriching experience for artists and audience members alike. Every city and town deserves the magical summer evenings that a flashlight-lit *Midsummer Night's Dream* filled with irreverently marauding fairies and conspiratorial lovers can bring. Read *Gorilla Theatre* and then go out and make some.

Martin Denton
editor-in-chief
nytheatre.com
NYC 2002

acknowledgments

After a Theatre Communications Group–sponsored talk at Pace University on directing Shakespeare, Arthur Bartow (artistic director at New York University's Tisch School of the Arts, Department of Undergraduate Drama) suggested that I write a book about the way I make theatre. I hope that he will be credited for any contributions that the book makes, and that its deficits will be debited entirely to me. His kind encouragement got the ball rolling.

Numerous Angels have reached down into my life to help make this book happen, and Mortals as well—too many to mention in one volume, let alone one acknowledgments page. Chief among the Celestial Host must be numbered Lila Rose Kaplan, who with the great patience and dedication of a true teacher has rescued this book from uncertain Fate time and time again. Speaking of time:

Once upon a time, I knew a man who flew back and forth from Washington, D.C., to New York all the time, recording his thoughts on and impressions of the Off-Off Broadway theatre productions he saw there. He put down these thoughts on a new medium in a readable format. And people paid attention, because they were excellent thoughts—well put and concise. Years later, all and sundry thank him for his honesty, his passion, and his untiring support of the art form of theatre. Martin Denton, of **www.nytheatre.com,** has gifted us all with a sense of community in troubled times, and many wonderful projects have been born in his (now relocated to New York) living room over cups of Rochelle's magnificent coffee.

Kathryn Walat, a brilliant playwright and writer, took the time to edit the Gorilla Rep Manifesto for **theatremania.com**, and I thank her for her patience and insight. It's the better for her efforts.

Most of all, the director would like to thank the casts and crews of all Gorilla Repertory Theatre Company shows for the donation of their untiring effort, uncompromising discipline, unshakable dedication, and unbelievable talent. They have made all of my *Midsummer Night's Dream*s come true.

The National Endowment for the Arts, New York City Department of Cultural Affairs, Department of Parks and Recreation, and The Laura Pels Foundation have helped the Gorilla Repertory Theatre Company, and I thank them here. Thanks to Commissioners Adrian Benepe and Schuyler Chapin. Ongoing thanks to the board of trustees and kind supporters of the Gorilla Repertory Theatre Company Foundation.

Thanks to original Gorilla Rep Board members Tom Bresnahan and John Rue, members Diane Magnuson and Adam Gulinello, and of course a Big Shout Out to John George Murphy III, the board's longest-serving and hardest-working president. Katherine Gooch was of indispensable help to Gorilla Rep throughout its birth and first decade, anchoring many shows with her unstoppable talent and work ethic. To Lynda Kennedy, thanks. All the "OG" Original Gorillas, thanks, especially Eric Dean Scott, Marla Stollar, and Ken Schatz. Thanks to Michael Laurence, Jesse McKinley, Tim Cusick, Jack Haley, and those who came together for the very first *Hamlet* paratheatrical rehearsal—you all had a lot to do with this book at its very roots, as did The Experimental Theatre Wing (ETW) at New York University's Tisch School of the Arts, Paul Langland, Mary Overlie, Wendel Beavers, the wise Master Teacher Steve Wangh, my directorial role model Kevin Kuhlke, Richard Schechner, and all of those who provided a hothouse for this work during its earliest stages. To Moises Kaufman, my big brother at ETW and the winner of all of our sibling rivalries. Raina Von Waldenburg, Katherine Linton, Kirk Marcoe, Alyssa Bresnahan, and all of my valuable early critics and colleagues helped my thinking about gorilla theatre. Christina Cabot's book *Acting as a Spiritual Discipline* was a guide and an inspiration. Sean Seibert, thanks for believing in *Henry V* and helping make it happen so well through some difficult times. The whole *Henry V* cast worked extremely hard and embraced the form of the paratheatric magically and effectively. Greg Petroff holds the record for most Gorilla Rep parts in one season (I think it's twenty) and probably the record for most Gorilla Rep parts, period. Eric K. Daniels, thanks. I'd like to especially thank William Germano, Gilad Foss, and Tenessa Gemelke at Taylor & Francis for their contributions to shaping this book. Marjorie Heins of the

ACLU deserves credit and thanks for rescuing *UBU IS KING!* in Grand Central in New York City. Phil Thurston, Brett Singer, and Peter and Alice Cromarty helped immeasurably to get the word out about us.

If The Center for Cultural Evolution up in Colrain gets in touch with you, you are very lucky. ReBekka Tippens, Firekeeper, hosts this excellent spot for paratheatrical rehearsal research. Ann Rue, Robert and Suzanne Sanderson, Mr. and Mrs. Tarbox, Matt and Pat Gorlay, and many others have generously supported this work by hosting paratheatric rehearsals and providing the grounds for them.

Those who let me stay with them helped to make this book happen. Most notably, I would like to thank Lily You and Michael Tollefson for their generous hospitality when I was in my final stages of writing, as well as Michael and Mary Jane Smith and their wonderful family. Yale University and Hamden Hall Country Day School, who hired me while I was working on the book—especially my senior colleague and advisor David Krasner, a brilliant author, theoretician, and actor (who must be dragged back onto the stage)—are to be warmly thanked. I would like to acknowledge the insight of my community of colleagues at the Undergraduate Theatre Studies Program and Graduate School of Drama at Yale University. Preeminent theatre scholar, director, and playwright Leonard Jacobs has my thanks for his objective advice and wisdom on the work. During the writing of this book, Mathey College at Princeton University and Davenport College at Yale University gave me faculty fellowships as an adjunct faculty member. I am currently a very grateful resident fellow of Jonathan Edwards College at Yale, and I wish to thank the Master and Associate Master, Gary and Sondra Haller, for their valuable and kind support.

Benjamin Heller's photographs have shown me things about the work that I wouldn't have seen without them, and I thank him for his tireless coverage of many Gorilla Rep seasons.

Anthony G. Sanderson built platforms and clever site modifications for some of the first paratheatric rehearsals and Gorilla Rep tour performances in beautiful Cumberland County, Virginia.

Matt Liepe was my first editor at New York Casting, and the lessons he taught me have stuck. I thank him for them.

In memoriam Ryszard Cieslak. You were the first actor to whom I offered the role of King Lear. Rest in peace—brilliant actor, kind friend, good teacher.

About Gorilla Repertory Theatre Company, Inc.

In 1989, a talented group of people came together to help me put on a production of William Shakespeare's *A Midsummer Night's Dream* in Washington Square Park, in the heart of New York City's Greenwich Village. It moved from place to place as it went from scene to scene around the southwest corner, near the asphalt hills, and bouncing over the playground fixtures there. The actors and a few helpful volunteers lit the show with flashlights.

When I watched that first audience of fifty or so intrepid New Yorkers go running after the actors to get the best spots for the next scene, I knew we were on to something. The show has run every summer since, to audiences numbering in the hundreds each night. I'm so thankful for the blessing of this show. It helped me launch an aesthetic and form a company that is now more than ten years old. This was the birth of gorilla theatre.

I have watched this aesthetic grow and inspire others to build on the ideas and forms that we have generated. From Gorilla Rep's work has come inspiration to groups in cities and on campuses all over the United States and the world. Here is a practical guide to that aesthetic.

If you are thinking about mounting such a show or have done so and want input from Gorilla Rep's years of work and the cat that dreamt up this crazy way of doing theatre, this book is for you. Welcome to gorilla theatre!

This book is a guide to creating gorilla theatre: productions that move from place to place as they go from scene to scene, in outdoor public spaces for the most part, and for free. Here is a look at the process that has generated so many shows and so much fun, and a study of how these ideas and values all fit together to enhance a production. It is also a suggestion that you all pool your marketing resources in a painless, productive way and call your work gorilla theatre. You can thereby associate yourselves with the company that started it all, and with each other's growing efforts. Who knows what the next step will be for this art form? Let's make this one together. This book is my effort to help you do so.

There is a cultural imperative that demands that we contribute to our culture, and this is my contribution. The river that is my culture in the broadest sense runs too wide and too deep for me to know it all, but I can feel the way it carries me. This is the tributary that my times demanded of me: free, outdoor theatre that moved from place to place as it went from scene to scene, most often of classical dramatic material, most often telling favorite stories in a new way. I have managed, with the help of many others, to bring this aesthetic to expression. I was lucky enough to sense that this expression was needed. And what felt like a risk—active theatre—might have simply been a response to the provocation of a passive culture.

We spend our time preparing for adventures that never happen; we buy startlingly large, rugged vehicles that we use for trips to the grocery store. We wear shoes built for running or hiking, and we use them to walk to these rugged vehicles and promptly drive away. Gorilla Theatre and its mode of production gives people something exciting to do of an evening; an adventure made up chiefly of some spirited walking around. But that walking around is informed by the audience's imagination. It is informed in a way that the disengaged forms of traditional theatre and art could never hope to duplicate. We walk through landscapes populated by what the best playwrights and the culture have to offer, presented with enthusiasm and joy by artists dedicated to their craft.

I say that the Theatre we all love is not made out of bricks and mortar. It is made out of two elements: the actors and the audience. When these two elements become one through performance, that one thing they form is the Theatre.

In gorilla theatre, as previously stated, the audience and the actors move from place to place physically as the play progresses from scene to scene. In this medium, the encounter between the actors and the audience is the most raw, the most dependent on the players and on the strength of the text. The audience and the actors have imaginations that need to be invoked and harnessed to the storytelling. They are both active in building the Theatre, right there and then. How many times have we been told that good listening is active, not passive? An audience listens with wider ears, wondering, on many levels, "What next?" The dynamic between the audience and the cast is intense, unlike anything I've seen or experienced before. And it translates into observable phenomena, in immediate terms.

An actor will often wonder, and with good reason, of the audience during a show, "Are they with us?" If a couple of hundred people get up and run to the next location, trying hard not to miss anything, believe me—they are with you.

Gorilla Rep Manifesto

By Christopher Carter Sanderson, founding artistic and producing director, Gorilla Repertory Theatre Company, Inc. (Reprinted by permission from **theatremania.com**.)

man-i-fes-to: a written statement declaring publicly the intentions, motives, or views of its issuer

Gorilla Repertory Theatre Company, Inc.'s mission is to provide the highest quality productions of classical dramatic material, with the flavor of contemporary immediacy, for people where they are, and free of charge. But why?

These are the reasons that I see:

1. Because participation in the highest forms of culture is a right and not a privilege. To speak the English language (even as a second language) is to inherit the cultural richness that it contains. This inheritance is celebrated and transmitted in the theatre in a way unlike that of any other medium. This inheritance should be as easy to participate in as it is to check out a book from the public library.

2. Because all theatre is political. And, therefore, we will make a political statement with every production that we create whether we intend to or not. This statement should be made responsibly and consciously and included in the very foundation of the mise-en-scène. It is as much a choice as any design decision is. More so. Gorilla Rep proposes a production of *Romeo and Juliet* staged in Harlem's Jackie Robinson Park, cast biracially along the family lines, and race-blind for the unrelated characters. Here, the focus is real, and it is on race issues in New York City right now. By the nature of its work and location, Gorilla Rep's work has a heightened political sensibility; it is art, in situ, in real society. It is designed to awaken the senses on many levels, political thought being one of them.

3. Because culture is dynamic by nature. The dialogue between classical works and current culture is inevitable, and we can accelerate and optimize this interaction by admitting it into the mise-en-scène itself. This artistic choice brings classical texts into a dialogue with current associations. The synthesis that arises is new thought, new feeling, new behavioral modes, and new freedom. Washington Square Park becomes a wood outside of Athens in *A Midsummer Night's Dream*, and then an orchard in Russia in *The Cherry Orchard*. Fort Tryon Park becomes an embattled Scotland in *Macbeth*, the *Peking*, docked at South Street Seaport Museum, becomes the ship and setting for *Pirates of Penzance* in Gorilla Rep's delightful staging. And Andre-Philippe Mistier transforms Washington Square Park yet again into the woods and courts of *As You Like It*, as it was once transformed into the blasted heath of *King Lear*. The imagination is invoked and given freedom and a framework for seeing quotidian settings in a new way. The public space has a collective purpose, and an individual impact.

4. Because we should let the Dinosaurs die. The value model for most modes of delivering theatrical participation is outmoded. Butts in seats are more valuable than eyeballs on sites. To be near the heart of these creations is to be near the hearts of the audience. It builds lasting loyalty and prestige for a brand or company. The old for-pay modes of theatre that survive the new age of free theatre will be influenced by the high standards of quality that exist in the new form.

5. Because we should eat the Dinosaurs. We must take advantage of the opportunity presented; the theatre is an undervalued medium for exchange of ideas and cultural production. The more we provide top-quality shows, the more we set the paradigm for decision and evaluation. People will choose to make this work a part of their lives, to take advantage of this conduit to participation in the culture. The more sincere our pumpkin patch is, the more likely it is that the Great Pumpkin will arrive. Our audiences are hungry to experience the work, to understand, to engage, to move and to grapple with it in a saturated and energized way.

And why does the gorilla aesthetic support this mission?

Let's use Shakespeare as an example. Shakespeare writes wonderful fiction, and it is my goal to surround these fictions with a creative world that serves their needs—the needs of the stories themselves. The important markers are there, in the text.

To place a Shakespearean play in a setting that is specific to a particular time period is to abdicate creative responsibility at the highest level: in short, it's a cop-out. It solves all of your design and direction questions with punctilious attention to "period detail" and ducks the real responsibility of building a milieu that gives the kind of richness of detail and contradiction that Shakespeare's plays present us with on the page. Go to a museum of frozen mannequins for your "period detail." As the characters live in their contradictions, the plays thrive in a polyanachronistic collage, stitched together from whatever works to evoke the correct supportive nuances.

Sometimes they are referential to specific cultural archetypes or shared images, sometimes referential only to the fantasy of the play. That said, this attention to detail should go all the way down to the pronunciations. In each instance, the pronunciations are the ones that I have experienced as true to my audience's ear: the ones that seem to best help them hear the meaning without stopping to process or "translate" it.

Shakespeare wrote English, there should be no need for such "translation" in your experience of his writing. So, if your English teacher told you that some of these words are pronounced differently from what you hear at a Gorilla Rep show—I suggest that you relax, hustle a bit between the scenes, and let the continuity of all of these interrelated choices entertain you for a while. Judge them on your way home (which often isn't far).

The essential Gorilla Rep manifesto is: Have fun now!

chapter one

Concept and Location

Inspiration

I have often said that the beginning of the process for me comes with the simultaneous realization of the play and location. The often-related story of the "Eureka Phenomenon" is one that plays well in the papers. However, on sober reflection, it is clear that an ambient, multilevel creative process is also at work. There is a lot of vocal warm-up that can be done, so to speak, before one shouts "Eureka!" from the rooftops.

Have ideas for multiple shows and sites milling around in your mind if possible. As you read plays and tour potential environments, partly formed notions should crop up in your imagination. Even one scene that erupts perfectly formed in your mind's eye as you walk around a park or other public place is a breakthrough. You are thinking gorilla style! Once a string of such scenes becomes clear, you probably have a full-fledged concept ready to talk about with your friends and collaborators.

Many creative notions start with one interesting bit. Andre Mistier's funky, enigmatic songs start with a lyric, even a phrase, or a few bars of succinct melody. Chris Barron's fantastic funk often starts with a memory or a person in mind, or a situation. Rob Hightower's brilliant, modern sculptures and evocative, spare paintings start with the most basic fascination with a technique or even a color. Each of these men, like a modern Mozart, Lord Byron, or Rodin, builds works of art that immediately take up residence in one's soul. This is my goal for gorilla theatre: a lease on the soul of this troubled culture. True, some concepts for gorilla theatre may leap from your brain fully formed like Athena from the brow of Zeus. Not every one will, though, and the clear, interesting idea should be seen as the tip of a mountain whose slopes lie under the sea, waiting to be discovered.

Also, it is worth noting down your play titles and sites as you go along. With each pair that has even a little "ah-ha" to it, something may develop later. They say that fortune favors the brave. I can say that fortune has favored this particular loudmouth by dropping the building blocks for some wonderful work right into my lap. But, each time, I had a play in mind and a site just perfect for it, so I could lay claim to whatever resource happened to present itself.

Macbeth at Fort Tryon Park is a fine example. I had been journeying up to the Cloisters in New York City's Fort Tryon Park for years. It is up north on 190th Street and has a wonderful view of the river. It was a place where I could go for just the price of a subway token and still feel like I had been out of the city for an afternoon. One day, thinking and walking around the park, I happened to wander up to the side of the battle monument, and the witches leapt into my mind, speaking down from the battlements over the archway. I walked through the arch to hear Duncan and his warlords discussing the battle, and then the witches led me down the hill to a tree, and the rest of the play flowed right along to the final claustrophobic constraint of Macbeth and the titanic battle on the nearby hill. When staged, the battle became truly titanic, as the 1K floodlights cast the shadows of the combatants onto the underside of the towering oak foliage canopy. It was like watching giants battle against the trees and evoked the impact of these moments on the history that would follow. It was three years before I could convince the Gorilla Rep board to set to work on this show, now one of our best known. The resource that dropped into my hands was in the form of a donor who, on hearing the idea, liked it enough to donate the funds we needed to get the job done.

Similarly, *Richard III* by the lake in Central Park had been knocking around in my mind for some time when the resources and personnel made themselves available. It was an easy call to make, as everything appeared to be present to make a gorilla-theatre show. The show spawned a whole new company to make gorilla-style theatre, which they did from time to time for a few years after that.

Talking about concepts is a way to make them take shape and grow, both in your mind and in reality. I have often launched a production with full force on the strength of one brilliant actor who is perfect for a role agree that it would be an exciting project to work on. So, talking to actors is important. Also, not every question about a show is a threat—thinking up the answers will help to flesh out the concept. The essential truth about directing is that selection is as creative a process as generation; you must select the ideas that enhance your concept with truly focused artistic concern. Think of what is best for the show from the perspective of the audience.

Of course, once you've fallen in love with the concept for a production at a specific site, you should nurture this feeling. Talk about it, especially at parties, although I recommend that you keep it to a three-sentence summary at first. Those who want to know more will ask, and this will sharpen your ability to communicate clearly and in a moving way just what is so exciting about your concept. This, incidentally, prepares you for offering short, punchy answers to the media when you're interviewed. People who love theatre in any way who are together for drinks, dinner, or whatever reason are an ideal group on whom to try out a concept, in measured doses. After all, if the idea isn't provoking anyone's imagination but yours, even you might wake up one day and realize that it was a bit limited or overly facile. It's all right to fall out of love with a concept; it happens. You never know—elements of that concept might help to flesh out a future plan.

Read Plays, Shakespeare First

Shakespeare's plays don't need further recommendation from me. They are beyond praise. They tell their stories strongly, clearly, and with wonderful layers of meaning and nuance—especially the ones done most often. What I do want to say is that Shakespeare, almost without exception, is the playwright whose work commends itself the most to outdoor, environmental, gorilla-style production. Although new plays are important to the form, I suggest that you perform a Shakespearean production first if you are pursuing this aesthetic.

Here are a few practical reasons for working with Shakespeare first. These reasons will give you a good framework for making decisions about directing new plays later. Shakespeare wrote plays for an unamplified environment. The texts, therefore, are seeded with devices specifically designed to be taken advantage of by an unamplified production. There is often restatement of key plot elements, often immediately following each other in the text. If you have an audience of more than a hundred people, you will quickly find that an actor can face a different direction for each of these expositions and get everyone well along in the story. Of course, the next layer of complexity is to weave and circle the actor back and forth between these areas so that every audience member gets every point clearly, but in a different order. This goes for scenes and their staging as well.

The often-cited fact that Shakespeare writes the scenery into his plays helps out too. Although this device has been used to advantage by minimalist scenic designers on empty modern sets, for your gorilla production these words can suggest far more to an audience. They can reveal that the skyscraper an audience is directed to look at is a castle, that the few sparse trees of your urban park are a magnificent forest, and so on. In short, Shakespeare's words can act as your scenic paintbrush to transform an entire environment many times during the play. Reread the prologue of *Henry V*, if you have not been lucky enough to see Jeffrey Kitrosser's effervescent performance of it, and think about a park. This should evoke the aesthetic very clearly, and in Shakespeare's words. The dedicated storytelling of a well-rehearsed gorilla-style actor will do more for your scenery than a fleet of bulldozers and landscape architects could.

Iambic pentameter supports acting; it gives an underlying pace not only to the flow of the story but to the very breath of the actors. You can put in breath marks the same way you would with a piece of choral music. That the characters think as they speak their lines and not during pauses allows the actor to look right into an audience's eyes and involve them in the story. The plays lend themselves to multiple casting of roles, and this, well done in the park, can be breathtaking. I am reminded again of the Gorilla Rep's *Henry V* in Northampton, Massachusetts. The audience members couldn't believe that we had only six members in the cast—they thought there were at least eighteen!

Other authors have proven durable and useful in gorilla-theatre shows. My personal bias against the ancient Greeks may be supported by noting that they are very short on action. You may be able to commission an adaptation of an ancient Greek tragedy or comedy, but I have yet to see one that really works. Beau Willimon's dramatic adaptation of *Beowulf* seems ideal for gorilla-theatre production. Perhaps, along these lines, you could create an adaptation of the *Iliad* or the *Odyssey*. Leah Ryan's adaptation of *The Cherry Orchard* for Gorilla Rep was a brilliant success, and I believe that other Chekhov plays, especially those in which the outdoors is an important part of the action, like *Ivanov*, could be well adapted for gorilla theatre.

Bottom (Bill Migliore), right, makes a friend. Photo by Lynda Kennedy.

In my experience, a playwright who hasn't seen a gorilla-theatre production is less likely to understand the needs of one than a playwright who has often been in the gorilla-theatre audience. Much like the gorilla actors, playwrights well suited to the work will usually enjoy a gorilla performance, and will later think, completely benignly, that what they saw was fun but that they could do it better. Still, I've been hotly approached by playwrights who have insisted that their work was perfect for the gorilla-theatre style who have then shown me plays that baffled me completely. The art of choosing a play for gorilla theatre is just that: an art.

Since premiering Talia Field's *The Celibate*, I have not directed a non-linear or "language" play. I directed *The Celibate* as an interior, environmental, or "action theatre" work, using many elements that would later become hallmarks of gorilla theatre. Chapter 12 contains a fuller description of this staging. My point is that I believe that gorilla theatre is not exclusively for producing "classic" dramatic material. I know otherwise, in fact. Perhaps classic material has been an easy choice, or a very practical one made to introduce gorilla theatre to the world. The future of the form may determine that it premiered classic work: contemporary work that became classic due to its widespread enjoyment and acceptance of gorilla-theatre audiences.

At first, a new play will need to be evaluated for relevance. Why would this play be better staged outdoors? Do the transitions between scenes—and hence from location to location—make sense? Why are they occurring? Shakespeare couldn't move his wooden "O" from place to place, and if we are going to move our audience around a park or through a city neighborhod all evening we should have good reasons for doing so. The audience must believe that the scene-location changes are logical textually. *The Zoo Story*, for example, is a play that has often been suggested as a Gorilla Rep production. But is it possible, really? I think to be truly gorilla, it would have to move from park bench to park bench, and I am not sure the playwright's text would support or be supported by this notion. One of the most amusing uses of the form to date has been "returning" to a location in the story that is being represented by an entirely different real site in the staging. Simple, but fun, as it can be used to underline the way that we look at the "place" that is represented in the story. What is the function of "place" in a language play? How does it fit the mise-en-scène, and what makes it work with dynamic moves from place to place? I believe that the future of gorilla theatre includes new plays, but not just any new play.

That's why it's essential that we work with playwrights right from the beginning of a project. "Support playwrights, not plays," as Ellen Stewart, founder of New York's La Mama, once said to me. When you find out that a playwright whose work you enjoy is interested in this form, it's time to think about commissioning a play.

List Plays

Keep a list of plays you have seen that have provoked you. Where, why, and how would you do them outdoors?

Your goal in gorilla theatre is the same as in any theatre in that you want to transport the audience into the world of the show. You want it to live around them, and for them to live in it. That's not to say that gorilla theatre is analagous to a scripted improvisation at a Renaissance Fair; in gorilla theatre the literary aspect of the text is key. The words are really important, and I don't want to lose sight of that, to use a Bottom-like malapropism. You use a behavioral metaphor to help carry the hearts and minds of your audience along the language that the playwright has provided, building durable characterizations and pointing up the dramatic action as you go.

The term *site-specific* is one that is often confused with *gorilla theatre*. Anne Hamberger and her famous, now defunct En Garde Arts organization in New York City brought the process of "site-specific theatre" to prominent and successful use. It was very specifically defined. It would begin with finding an exciting nontheatrical space such as an old hospital, or the Federal Building on Wall Street. Then a playwright would be commissioned to write a new play specifically for performance in that space. The history and character of these contemporary sites informed the plays, even when they were not exactly linear stories. With few exceptions, En Garde would build theatre-style seats into their sites, making possible the standard theatrical practice of charging for tickets before the performance, which of course is not the way gorilla theatre is done. So, when we talk about commissioning plays for gorilla theatre, we're not necessarily talking about "site-specific" work. If it moves from place to place as it goes from scene to scene, and if it has a particular depth of direction and facility of performance without pause or condescension, it may well be gorilla-theatre-style directing.

The "site-specific" aesthetic's goal, and it is a laudable one, is to point up the nature of the actual place that has been chosen for the play. An old hospital or a prerenovation theatre, the Bow Bridge in Central Park or wherever, the play pointed at the place. With gorilla theatre, the effect of pointing up the beauty of the location occurs, but we are interested in transporting the imagination by transforming the location into someplace fantastic and other than what it is. Fort Tryon Park starring in the role of Illyria, or New York City featured in the role of ancient Athens, Scotland, or the Russian countryside, is one way of thinking of the role of the place in gorilla theatre. Camp Shohola's soccer field becomes both the city-state of Athens and the haunted grove nearby as easily and magically as the armory in Scranton does. It is a valuable way of thinking when you are conceiving a gorilla-theatre production, because it will help you place your show with care and with a fully articulated vision. It is also a notion that has, happily, occurred to professional critics writing about Gorilla Rep.

With this idea in mind, you can be the first to look at a particular public space in a new way: the way your gorilla show will guide many people to see it. The sign of a good, clear vision is the feeling, fully supported, that you have been to the show and enjoyed it, after paying close attention to the performance. This feeling should be evident weeks or months before the show opens. As I have noted, the essential technique is to project your mind through time to the performance and look around with as much clarity as you can conjure until you have a clear idea of what you are building, no matter how unlikely it may seem to the world at large. It will be interesting and novel when it finally happens, no matter the intervening exigencies of day-to-day life.

All of the true principles of real, living theatre are alive and well in the scene-sites of a gorilla theatre layout. In the production of *Cymbeline* that I directed in Riverside Park, for instance, natural slopes provided great and varied sight lines. These sloped areas had natural frames of foliage in different formations that could be pointed up for the action. Even the cave area was a little more sharply raked, as Brian O'Sullivan will confirm if asked. It was also well carpeted with thicker hillocks of grass that, as Brian had the audience writhing in laughter, helped to cushion their manic gyrations. If his characterization could have been any more fun, I'm sure I don't know how, and this funny, funny character bounding around in the remote cave was accentuated by the higher hill. The slope helped speed Jo Benincasa's exit after brandishing the sword he had just taken from Tom Staggs's Cloten, and there was darkened foliage right there to muffle the screams of the comic death "offstage." And there was much ruffling of that foliage in death throes', to add to the hilarity. The rocks were a literal aid, but I believe it was the steep rake that really brought a masterful stroke to the isolation of the place in the story.

What fantastical environment does the public space seem best to represent? It might help to think of the park as an actor—in the next section, we'll talk about *Alice In Wonderland*, and how Federal Plaza was perfectly dressed for the role of Wonderland. Your public space, the one where you are thinking of producing a gorilla-theatre show—what role is it asking to play? Some answers are easy: Bethesda Fountain in Central Park, for example, is begging to play Venice in *The Merchant of Venice*. (Unfortunately, Bethesda Fountain is reserved for events and film companies that can pay millions of dollars for the privilege to use it, and the Constitutional rights of freedom of speech and freedom to assemble are suspended in this particular part of Central Park.) Sometimes the answer is not as easy, and it will be completely elusive if the space doesn't have ample provision for the audience around each scene-site. However, if the is right, the answer will come; you need only spend time at the site, preferably while reading plays.

Tour Sites

People often tell me about possible gorilla-theatre locations. I welcome these suggestions or commissions now, and I also get around and look at the architecture around me. For an example of how to observe the potential of gorilla theatre in a city, read *The Fall of Public Man*, by Richard Sennett. It contains a useful historical perspective on the current lack of collective use of public land. I was on my way to court in New York City (don't ask me why) on one blustery, beautiful spring day when I happened to take a shortcut around a corner and walked right into Federal Plaza. An uninspiring name, I agree, but it turned out to be an amazingly inspiring site for a wonderful production of *Alice in Wonderland*. The little park there, which I later learned was built to give the federal employees a nice place to eat lunch, was divided by the most evocative humps of well-tended bright green grass. There wasn't a straight line in the place; even the benches were long, serpentine, and looped, naturally enclosing potential audience areas. This loopy, surreal space, so neat and proportional, was dominated by a series of giant picturesque gas-lamp poles. Of course, the lights weren't really antique gas-operated ones. They were modern and electric and provided a very useful ambient light, which we augmented with the trademark Gorilla Rep flashlights. It all came to me in a flash, so to speak. The vision bound the ambient elements—light poles, benches, grassy hills—into a coherent whole.

Washington Square Park is conveniently located between Carmine Street and Waverly in Greenwich Village. In 1989, I was living on Carmine while attending New York University's Tisch School of the Arts, whose undergraduate theatre department houses the Experimental Theatre Wing on Waverly. I happened upon the location for *A Midsummer Night's Dream* by luck. I was ready to do a comedy, and *A Midsummer Night's Dream* seemed like the best one to do, but I wasn't sure which space would be right for it. Then I walked over a hill and saw the whole show unfold in my mind's eye, and it was set right there in Washington Square Park. That show is still running.

Other sites take longer to grow, and I don't want to give you the illusion that every one of my visions has been fulfilled. As I have said, Beau Willimon's adaptation of *Beowulf* is an example of a show and a location that I put together before there was a script. This was true of Leah Ryan's *The Cherry Orchard* as well, but that came together faster—in about a year once she had signed on. With *Beowulf*, the location is also a question mark in terms of availability. The Cop Cot is situated perfectly on the top of a small rise just off Central Park South. But it is a designated "quiet area" reserved for quiet reading, tête-à-têtes, and nodding off more than it is promoted as a nice place for gorilla theatre. Perhaps the park officials will come around, or perhaps we'll deal directly with the police. For now, I can tell you that, on the sunny afternoon of July 20, 2002, a group of actors met informally at the Cop Cot for a first reading of Beau's first draft. *St. Mary's Catholic Girls School English 201 Class Presents Romeo and Juliet* was halfway through its initial run at the Naumburg Bandshell, *A Midsummer Night's Dream* and *Henry V* were set to open in Washington Square Park in three weeks, and we would have loved to see *Beowulf* come together too. I pulled off *The Death of King Arthur* in Central Park as a late-season addition, but with arts money drying up it would be another year or more before I could build a Grendel puppet for *Beowulf*.

Bridges are the one point of geography that never seem to support gorilla theatre. It is an understandable temptation to want to stage scenes on bridges. They are usually beautiful places to look from, and to look at. However, they invariably fall under the category of scene-sites that do not allow adequate room for an audience. This is the trap of sites that look great in this way—like a movie set, they don't have any room for spectators.

As you investigate sites, bear in mind that attitudes toward public spaces in America have changed in the wake of the attacks on September 11, 2001. Your potential site may or may not be affected by this, but it is worth considering. Greg Petroff had been after me for years to create a Gorilla Rep show for the World Financial Center's Winter Garden Atrium. Having played everything from one of the "Mechanicals" in *A Midsummer Night's Dream* to Cornwall in *King Lear* to the lead role in *Macbeth* with Gorilla Rep, Greg knows the demands of the aesthetic. It was not until I toured the site, very early in the morning on September 11, 2001, that I fell in love with the image of tennis balls cascading down the elegant marble stairs there. (I had an early appointment in Princeton, so I toured the site and was on a train out of the city by 8 A.M.) Obviously, opportunities have changed since that day. The Federal Building where we premiered *Alice in Wonderland* and where we did performances for the federal employees' kids there couldn't allow us to return after the Oklahoma City bombing—the rules had changed. It is too early to know with certainty how gorilla theatre will be affected in the long run; the shows in the parks have gone off without a hitch, but the general atmosphere is certainly different.

A final item to take into account when selecting a gorilla-theatre location is the behavioral topography, if you will, of the location. These features will have as much to do with influencing the audience's perception as any foliage or lighting concerns will. For example, in the course of putting together *St. Mary's Catholic Girls School English 201 Class Presents Romeo and Juliet* in Central Park, we encountered a specific feature of the nearby space: a drumming group that regularly performed in the site. This caused a bit of consternation on the part of cast and crew at first, but I kept an iron countenance and firmly made sure that all elements for the performance were put in place. Sure enough, at exactly the time appointed by their permit, the punctual drummers stopped playing; our show went on in the new hush that dropped over the area. It was as sharp a behavioral spotlight as the ambient environment could afford. It was magic, and the show went well on that and every night that we followed the drummers. What else happens at your proposed location, who does it, and how do these uses influence the thinking about the park? The next question is: How can this be used to your show's best advantage? Does it affect staging, design, or timing? There's a lot of inspiration to be found in the living, collective, and individual uses of public space.

List Sites with Pros and Cons

Even that which appears as a negative mark at first may mesh with your resources at a later time. It is important to record as much as possible about the sites you are visiting. In fact, a location that you enjoy visiting but that doesn't click regarding a particular production may be the perfect place for a different show. The more locations you visit and the more plays you read and see in other venues, the wider the spectrum for the possibilities to mesh in your mind.

In a way, the site is a set. If you conceive of your audience as part of your cast and imagine a satisfying, well-paced experience overall, this will help guide your process of site selection. Often, as you walk past a statue or walk through a public atrium, you may begin to associate scenes and staging. This is good—nurture this visioning. But don't stop there; ask yourself about the next step: Can an audience fit around the action? Can you see, from here, where the next scene needs to occur? And how would the audience get there from here? Would it be fun?

Allow the focus of your attention on the site to range in and out along the scales of time and place. In time, the atmosphere builds from

Audience in Area B during Macbeth in Fort Tryon Park, New York City, June 2000. Photo by Benjamin Heller.

the audience members' first exposure to an ad or any listing mentioning the show—truly, from their first exposure to the fact of the show's existence. Also space—what distance are they covering to get there, and how will they be doing it? A public park in New York City benefits from proximity to the subway; in Los Angeles, you need a park with lots of convenient parking. All of the pieces need to fit together—from travel to flow to what kind of weather you anticipate. The more variables and elements that you are aware of, the better. This includes the history of the city, both recent and distant, and of the park itself. If you know the importance of Calvert Vaux in the design of Central Park and have seen old engravings, for instance, you will design better shows for Central Park and won't be seduced by the simple fact that the park is famous.

The risk/return ratio on your early experiments with gorilla theatre should be considered in terms of difficulty of getting to the site. One day, I will drop out of an airplane with fifteen or twenty other crew and actors (more about zero-gravity staging later) and put on a production in the pristine Alaskan wilderness for a very select audience. In the meantime, more accessible areas help in at least two ways. One is the obvious fact that people recognize that travel to and from the location will not be a problem or an inconvenience. But the less obvious guarantee of quality is also present: an easily accessible site is also an easy site to get away from if you don't like what you are experiencing. "The exits are clearly marked," as I often say to people who find themselves wishing to leave the hurly-burly brilliance of New York. And for an audience member who might have shown up at a gorilla-theatre show expecting a plush seat and every other traditional-theatre amenity, a clear way out will be as much appreciated as the way in.

Isolation can be an advantage, however, if the location is not too far away from the main population center in your area. Fort Tryon Park is not the most accessible of New York City parks, until you get used to going there. But the quiet and the isolation from the noise of the rest of the city make it a wonderful setting for gorilla theatre. Battery Park is also not a major tourist destination on most nights at 8:00 P.M. The traffic noise is minimal there, and those who make the journey are rewarded with an undisturbed place to play. Both of those locations bring associations to mind for the audience, which allows them to make the "ah . . ." connection in their own minds before they make the trip. This connection happens at a more accessible spot that is nonetheless not as well known. There is a subtle difference between the thought in advance "that would be a great spot for that play" and the thought "hey, this is a great spot for this show." With *Beowulf*, for instance, I don't anticipate that many people know of the hidden mead-hall of the Cop Cot, even though it is only a block from busy Central Park South.

I think that the greatest danger to the gorilla-theatre aesthetic is trying to turn it into something that it is not and expecting the same dynamic energy. There are wonderful productions to be created with sumptuous banquets served first and servants to run behind the select crowd, or even charge-for-experience shows that move around like golf. They may be interesting, and they may be lucrative, and they may be enjoyed by those who can afford to pay the ticket prices, but these shows are gorilla theatre. Gorilla theatre is a populist theatrical movement first, no matter how highbrow the content at times, and no matter how far ranging its influence. This is a key factor of the aesthetic.

This fact plays into the selection of concept and location in a number of ways. The magic of transforming a familiar park into the unfamiliar scenes of the story is an extraordinary enhancement to the drama itself. It surrounds the drama with another, framing drama, and this drama extends into the very lives of the audience. Even a tourist from far away will recognize this, and feel it as a part of the show. Local beers are famous, local food is well known, and your gorilla theatre, fully articulated into the local culture, will be seen in much the same light. There is nothing quite like watching a couple arrive with basket, wine, and blanket in tow, with a smug, comfortable look, knowing that they are about to add to their cultural vocabulary in a way nobody warned them about. Then to see the smiles as they tuck into their slightly delayed repast after the show with much more to talk about than a mellow summer concert would have provided. That's gorilla theatre!

chapter **two**

Scouting

Organizations That Can Help

Gorilla Rep shows have been helped, in part, by many government institutions. A common mistake is considering "funding" to mean only "cash donations." But there is so much more that needs to be given to create a gorilla-style show. The permission and cooperation of the people who are responsible for the site in which you are working are among the most important requirements of producing a gorilla show, and usually that has nothing to do with money. It takes time and patience to get the attention of these busy, often overworked people, but their help is worth earning. If not for them and their staffs, you would be looking at a derelict site and you'd be faced with problems you hadn't even dreamed of. An untended urban space invites security and safety problems for you and your crew and cast. It will also frighten away a large segment of your prospective audience unless you intend to attract only real urban commandos. By the way, the commando audience is cool, but my experience has been that they consider their risk taking to be their price of admission and therefore won't donate much to the hat at the end of the show.

There are often signs around a public or park area indicating how to contact the group that keeps the area maintained. In my experience, a private group will be a bit more difficult to negotiate with than a public agency. This is for good reason; a private organization is more like a private landlord, with no real need to encourage any change in the status quo. They might respond to a monetary offer, but partnership isn't in their best interest if the risk is entirely theirs. You may be able to compensate for this by naming them in your insurance policy, but a private organization will still need a more compelling reason to go along with your plans than contributing to the cultural good.

Unfortunately, a fantastic dramatic concept is not often such a compelling reason. If a member or benefactor of the private organization is on your team, he or she would be the person to pick for approaching the organization about gaining permission to use their space. Or, initially, a fund-raising event for the organization with an abbreviated version of your full concept might be a good way to introduce it.

Governmental and public agencies have established forms for approaching the permit or permission process. If you are working on federal land, you will need to speak with some security experts at some point. I have found them polite and thorough, and they let me know whatever simple steps I can take to make our work together the most efficient it can be.

Gorilla Rep has more often worked with local agencies, usually the New York City Department of Parks and Recreation. They have been an extraordinarily helpful partner in Gorilla Rep's work in many ways over the years. The permit process in New York is smooth and consistently administered. Being prepared to go through it, and any permit process, is your responsibility. You will need (at minimum):

- Insurance coverage
- Specific dates and times for shows, set-up, and clean-up
- Permission for on-site rehearsals if you are planning them
- A plan for sanitary facilities for you and your audience
- A plan for any dressing areas necessary and required by Actors' Equity

You will also need to contact Actors' Equity and get a copy of the appropriate guidelines for working with union members. If you are casting nonunion members for some reason, the basic "Showcase" code is still a good, basic primer on how to set guidelines for the safety and comfort of all personnel.

There are a few ways to contact a permit agency initially, but I would use the following sequence from Gorilla Rep's efforts over the years as a good template to work from. A good way to start is to call the permit agency and find out the name of the person responsible for evaluating permit requests. Then send a short (less than a full page) letter to that person, along with a one-page summary of press quotes about your past work or quotes about similar work to provide context. Next, if you can find a friendly board member, or if you are working with a producer, they should book a brief meeting with the decision maker. Have them bring copies of full reviews and press about your past shows, or a more fully fleshed-out proposal. This proposal should include details on the entire checklist of concerns above, a list of people working on the project, a cast list (or a list of parts if the show isn't cast yet), and any design photos or sketches that you and your design staff have come up with. The purpose of this meeting should be to answer any questions about the organization and its general operating principles and procedures. Having this information when meeting with an official helps the organization to be fully informed when the director comes in to talk about details and agreements. And that's the next step.

As you are discussing the work that you'd like to do at the site in question, a good way to start is to ask what the official in charge would like to gain from the event. Does the organization have a mission to help bring more cultural opportunities to the community? Would they like to have a good reason for folks to visit their location? Do their employees have children who might attend the show? This will often lead into discussion of details like security, insurance, and other practical matters. If the conversation starts by including the goals of the site and its parent organization, these details will most often resolve themselves very clearly. Of course, as with any meeting in which agreements are reached, you will want to keep a record of your understanding of these agreements.

A follow-up letter should be sufficient to summarize the conversation, with any specific agreements bulleted for clarity. If the agreements entail paying any sums of money that seem significant to you or your organization, I recommend having the letter notarized and sending it by registered mail. This in itself is usually enough to flag the document for forwarding to the legal department of the organization. This is actually a good thing; it is better to have lawyers troubleshoot an agreement beforehand than to have it disputed later in court.

In less urban places, the forces that can help you create a gorilla-theatre production are more concentrated. Northampton, Massachusetts is a good example: the city cedes permit responsibility for the park outside Town Hall to the Arts Council. My experience is that a small town will want to see a show before agreeing to help you with much. This makes sense—there are lots of bad groups soliciting them all the time. And, as will anyone who hasn't experienced a gorilla-theatre show, they will want to see proof that it works. It is an idea that always sounds good, but one that needs to be experienced to be understood and supported properly. For example, we took our production of *Henry V* into Northampton, as we had a paratheatric rehearsal going on in nearby Colrain. The Arts Council learned about us, we were invited to perform, and I moved our rehearsal schedule to accommodate the request. I then approached the Arts Council for sponsorship—that is, some money to pay the actors and myself and so on—but their response was indicative of what can happen. They were happy to offer us a sponsorship—by waiving the fee for performing! So be prepared to give your potential sponsors a taste of your quality ahead of time if you expect sponsorship dollars. The situation is dire enough with dwindling arts funding, but with the current malaise afflicting large companies, nobody is going to trust you unless you show them what you can do.

In New York City, I've had better luck with institutions that had direct benefits to reap from cooperation. We've gotten giveaway items with company logos printed on them, and we've had ticket-selling Web sites set up for free, because the Web site would benefit from the traffic. Gorilla Rep did sell tickets once, for a performance of *Pirates of Penzance* that was staged at South Street Seaport's tall ship *Peking*. Conceived as a fund-raising effort, it merely broke even, though the distinctive gorilla-theatre staging drew lines circling the block every night and though the people in charge of the music and choreography worked at rates far below the usual Broadway range. In terms of helpful organizations, the museum that runs South Street rates very high, and I would suggest looking for historic sites that are this well managed as potential gorilla-theatre sites.

New York's ART, the Alliance of Resident Theatres, provides resources and classes on many areas of building and maintaining a not-for-profit theatre company. Although not particularly suited to all of gorilla theatre's goals and needs, this and organizations like it—such as TCG, the Theatre Communications Group—provide essential education and information to the theatre community.

Local schools can be a source of help. I have found that high schools in particular have students who are beginning to understand gorilla theatre. Certainly, schools have rehearsal space and volunteers, and they are a place where barter for these things can have meaning. The difficulty of working with schools begins when they start talking about doing shows for the students during school hours. Now, there is no deadlier audience than a captive audience, and I find the idea of forcing students to go to the theatre to be a horrible one. If there is a reason why the theatre is hated by some, this might be the root of it. Who wants to go to a show that is so bad that its audience needs to be forced to go see it? The relatively easy money of these student shows, and children's theatre as well in many instances, have lured many resources and many good creative personnel away from theatre for wider audiences. What makes sense to an elementary school teacher does not necessarily make for good theatre, much less good gorilla theatre.

Universities have discovered gorilla theatre through their students' interest. Although Gorilla Rep is included in the curriculum for many theatre survey courses, it is the students who have led the drive to create gorilla theatre. Student organizations may be the best places to start a gorilla-theatre production at your school. New York University, through the kind offices of Arthur Bartow, granted Gorilla Rep a special summer rehearsal-space residency that provided the platform on which to rehearse a number of shows over the years. Outside New York City, summer finds many schools with space available for workshops, residencies and, I would suggest, gorilla-theatre companies. Yale's undergraduate theatre studies program allowed three seniors to pool their resources to produce *Othello* there under my direction. I moved the production to New York City as a Gorilla Rep show, and it did very well at Central Park's Summit Rock.

Other organizations that can help include professional fund-raising companies or consultants. They should be approached cautiously. I will not dwell on their relative merits or demerits, as I have not found one to date that could handle gorilla theatre, despite the form's widespread positive reception by the public.

Rights of Free Speech and Assembly

The Constitution guarantees you the rights to freedom of speech and of public assembly. On the subject of organizations that can help you, the American Civil Liberties Union must be mentioned. When anyone is infringing on your rights, the ACLU can help. When a park official wishes to ban your performance entirely, the ACLU will work with you to help explain the situation to the park official and, if necessary, help you go to court to defend your rights. Designated public space is space where your rights exist in full, and it is useful to know this about one particular spot—public atriums of large office buildings. These office buildings receive tax breaks from the municipal government for maintaining these "public" spaces, but the government does not require them to advertise the fact that they are public. One aspect of their public nature is that planning for performances there needs to allow adequate lead time so that necessary permits can be filled out and submitted. Often, a company in the building will take advantage of the atrium to schedule lunchtime concerts for their employees; this does not take the place of allowing the public to perform there. These are the facts that led me to book our production of *Henry V* into the Winter Garden Atrium of the World Financial Center in 2001. It was to open September 23.

The first production of *UBU IS KING!*—the one-act adaptation of Alfred Jarry's *Ubu Roi*—had a troubled beginning. Now, years later, it has seen numerous productions, including one in Brazil, one with Lollapalooza, and many by Gorilla Rep in New York City. The first production was scheduled for Grand Central Terminal (as audience members pointed out, it is called Grand Central Terminal—not station—because the train lines end there). It was almost the end of *UBI IS KING!* as well, but it proved to be the beginning of Gorilla Rep instead.

I had directed *A Midsummer Night's Dream* in Washington Square Park every summer since 1989, and this was now 1992. I had moved on from a previous company to concentrate on work—always the best tonic for troubled times. The work in this case was *UBU IS KING!*, and I set out to write the adaptation and then cast and rehearse the show. Our first speed bump was learning about permits in Grand Central—our preview performance in early December was shut down about halfway through when the police learned that we didn't have a permit. So we applied and received our permit, and we returned. It was late January when we came back.

This time, we got through our opening performance quite well. It was a Friday-night crowd, about half of whom were downtown types and the other half commuters, some of whom had stayed after work and came by with their ties hanging loose. *UBU IS KING!* tells the story of Ubu in only one act, reducing the running time of the original play to about an hour. Anyone who has sat through the five acts of the original might see the mercy in this notion. Five acts of the same fart joke, as historically important as it is, is still five acts of the same fart joke. I wanted to design an *Ubu* that everyone, whether they claimed to have seen the original or whether they knew its importance but couldn't bring themselves to sit through a production of it, could watch and enjoy. That Friday night, it looked like we had succeeded in doing just that.

But the Saturday matinee was another story. We were working for a sizable crowd. This time, in addition to people who had come in just for the show, mostly from downtown, we also had some people in expensive suits stop by. I guessed that they were lawyers, on their way in to do some work on a Saturday. They had cashmere overcoats, leather briefcases, and nice shoes. Well, we always like a heterogeneous audience.

The show was going well. Each of the ten scenes was punctuated by a snare-drum beat as the actors—five men and five women—switched off the Ubu costume. This costume consisted of a mask with a long, pointy nose, a pointed hat, and a set of gigantic white buttocks and a three-foot-long phallus that swung around as the actor moved. The thing was stuffed as thick as a drainpipe and was ridiculous. An actor could get laughs just by walking around in it. This was all traded back and forth easily as the actors all wore white sweat pants and T-shirts. The actors were well trained and well rehearsed, and it was fun to see the whole idea, then more than a hundred years old, entertaining an audience.

My original dramaturgy should be mentioned here. It was simple—I wanted to cause a riot by telling this story the way it was intended to be told, as Alf Jarry had back in Paris almost a hundred years earlier. Now, direct provocation of the audience might have done this, but I thought it would just alienate them. At any rate, the police had helped *A Midsummer Night's Dream* in Washington Square Park stay safe, so I had no worries on that front. I thought that maybe, just maybe, the story itself, plus a squirt bottle of brown tempera paint and some whoopee cushions, would cause a stir.

That stir started during the second performance on Saturday. As we performed, I glanced over to my left and saw a man who had a large pot belly and a stark white crew cut. I had to look twice—I thought he was part of the show. A competing Ubu from across the station? I quickly realized that this was no joke, nor was the man a spillover from another show, as the assistant station master walked into the middle of the performance, started shouting for us to stop, and told us that our show was "obscene."

The scene that followed seemed suspended in time. Like a moment in some kind of Brecht play from Hell, I had three groups yelling at me: The assistant station master, with his crowd of blue shirts and badges, was demanding that we shut down the production or be arrested—or worse. On the other side, our sedate, gray-haired lawyers had taken up the chant "Fuck the Pigs!" (I guess they had all been activists once upon a time.) On the third side, the actors had huddled together in a protective knot and were tentatively but forcefully asserting their position that I should consult them before I made any major decisions.

Well, I shut down the show, took the names and numbers of those audience members who would give them, and assured them that we'd be back. My actual faith in that assertion was shaky, but it would improve as the week went on.

On Monday, the head critic for the *Village Voice*, Michael Feingold, called; I forget how he had heard of the incident, but by the end of the conversation I had a battle plan together, and I put it right into effect. His assertion was that, for better or worse, I was on the front line of the battle over freedom of speech, and I'd better damn well do something about it or all Art would suffer. I got on the phone and didn't get off until Marjorie Heins, the founding director of the ACLU's national anticensorship efforts, was taking our case personally. God bless her. She later wrote a brilliant book on the subject titled *Sex, Sin, and Blasphemy: A Guide to America's Censorship Wars*. By Wednesday, the Living Theatre, which then had a space on Second Avenue, had offered us a weekly Sunday-afternoon performance slot until we were "out of exile." God bless them, too. By Friday, Grand Central's legal forces were on the run, with faxes flying and rallying cries coming from all sides of the artistic world—and victory was in sight. The *Village Voice* kindly covered the fracas for three weeks running, and by the end of it I had "emerged" as an artist.

We retooled the show for our new permit, granted for a month later in a last act of attempted attrition by the forces of censorship, and it went on to great success. How did this show lead to the formation of the Gorilla Rep company? During the retooling process, I broached the idea that this aesthetic could fuel a company, and founding company member Amo Gulinello agreed. If memory serves, he thought up the name over tea and coffee at Café Borgia on MacDougal Street. I thought it was brilliant—everyone would ask if it was spelled "gorilla" or "guerilla," and it would stick in their minds that way. It worked because we were big, hairy, and smelly, but people seemed to like us anyway. As it turned out it became not only the name of a company, but also, now, a recognized term describing a theatre aesthetic.

Working Conditions for the Actors and Personnel

As you move around the environment, staking out the sites for each scene and remembering to envision a space in each for the audience, it is important to keep the working conditions of the actor in mind. Everything from travel time to sanitary facilities, changing-room needs, and so on should be considered well in advance. Exits and entrances will need to be considered as techniques as much as parts of the set—remember always that the great danger is to try doing indoor theatre outdoors. The aesthetic is unforgiving in this way, and the amateurish nature of such endeavors is only multiplied by this fact. There is a fresh, alive quality about gorilla theatre that draws audiences, who tell friends and bring more people to experience them. Some of this has to do with the conditions that the actors work under.

The actors must be coached in their attitude as much as anything. I have seen one attempt at gorilla style that was unsuccessful largely due to the fact that every time the actors ran "offstage" they would then look around in an embarrassed manner, as if they had been caught naked. This created a feeling of embarrassment around all of the action. It was uncomfortable for the audience. The director made quite a spectacle of herself by vigorously writing down notes just about every time a misstep occurred. Her angst-ridden performance soundly upstaged the poor struggling actors onstage.

A basic working condition for the actors that is even more important than a set of clean bathrooms is this: directors who rehearse them adequately and know what they are doing. Or directors who at least know how to be honest and who work harder when they don't know what they are doing. If your director doesn't do this, you'd better find one who does. Or, even better, be one.

In terms of scouting, a space that really makes an actor go "ah!" is a great place to work. Think of this: Who wouldn't say "ah!" and feel this way about the original Globe Theatre in London? Quite beyond being Shakespeare's own venue, it is a truly well-designed and acoustically warm space. Set your goal high: Make it your aim to excite actors as much as they would be excited about walking into the Globe. A good gorilla actor exclaiming, "Wow! We're doing it here? Where are my scenes?" is a good indication that your play is a successful match with the space. There are real, wooly, wild spaces, even some designed ones, that will be perfect.

You may find an exception, but I have found it better to change the costume design than to put up a changing tent or provide a truck to change in. In the end, the kind of embarrassment that comes from changing in a too-small tent is corrosive to the full gorilla-theatre confidence that you need. The model of a good performance is a small, self-contained unit of people and an empty park. Then, an amazing gorilla-theatre show. Then, an empty park again. In and out clean, with rock 'n' roll in between! Everything you do to optimize the space should, to the extent possible, be noninvasive to its original nature.

Mapping the Site

I have found creating a photo essay of the environment I am working in to be valuable. Especially when the problem of time needs to be turned into an asset, the well-executed photo essay pinned up around your work-room can be a great help as you mull over the behavioral sculpture that is a gorilla-theatre production. My basic photo essay consists of two parts. The first is a panorama, and the second is a three- or four-point shot of each scene-site. These are pretty straightforward shots and don't end up looking particularly inspiring—until you imagine the action taking place in them. For the panorama, I stand in one spot that has a view of all of the scenes. Keeping in mind that I need some overlap in the frames, I slowly revolve, snapping pictures as I go. The idea is to make one long line of overlapping shots that depicts the entire playing area from one point of view. If this can't be achieved, you could do it from two or even three points of view. One seems best to me, and it has worked well, as it indicates a coherent playing area that an audience can feel as a spacial frame for the show; something like a sports playing field. Someday, perhaps, playing fields will be constructed for gorilla theatre, but in the meantime I guess we'll be strictly sandlot. (Well, a sandlot would be a good place for *The Tempest*.) The second set of shots in the photo essay is of each scene-site, carefully placed from the representative points of view of the audience. Three or at most four shots are usually enough, and it should help you visualize the staging as you work on the show.

You also need to construct a schematic diagram, a clearly drawn guide for the actors. Each scene-site should be indicated, as well as the basic staging orientation (see chapter 6). These should be indicated by simple, easy-to-read symbols, as on the most basic of maps. Trees, major

The ensemble as the Apparition rushes up in *Macbeth* at Fort Tryon Park, New York City, June 2000. Photo by Benjamin Heller.

topographical features, and anything that will help to orient the actor are valuable. If bathrooms are present on the location, indicate where they are or in which direction. The same goes for water fountains, which can be of great service during a show on a hot, steamy evening. The strategy for lighting—whether it will be from power tapped from a source on location, or if a generator (which can be loud) will be installed each night, or if a truck is to be parked nearby—should be indicated, as it will have an impact on how the lighting design will be deployed each night. If there are major modifications to the scene areas—such as a huge plush rug or other scenic enhancement that will affect the work—it is good to have them indicated on the map or site-layout diagram as early in the process as possible. The actors will each be adding his or her own notes about transitions and stand-by areas on the main diagram, so it should not be a busy or overly florid depiction—it is a working tool for the actors and design team, and it should be about as creative in its depiction of the site as a blueprint of the light plot for an indoor show. An actor like Eric Daniels, who can pull off a wonderful dauphin in *Henry V*, amuse audiences with several comic roles, and hold down both some French and some English lords all at the same time, all with a the degree of skill that has audiences thinking he is multiple actors, is going to want to plan out all of his transitions clearly and simply, so that he can concentrate on the task at hand: brilliant acting. A simple indication of the direction "north," as on any map, will be useful at first, until the team is accustomed to the area.

What will be most useful on the diagram or map is a coding system for the scene-sites that the whole team can use as a shorthand when describing them. In most instances, I have simply named them alphabetically in the order of use. This has rarely gone past the letter "F." *Macbeth* in Fort Tryon Park had six playing areas that were used for the bulk of the play, while the first two scenes and the last act had sites of their own. The first and the final areas served as a way in and out of the pattern that *Macbeth* weaves. There is an area that is never used for an interior of Macbeth's castle—instead the scenes there are Banquo's murder, and later England with Malcolm and Macduff. There is an area where all of Lady Macbeth's scenes occur—area "D," nicknamed "Lady M's House"—with the exceptions of the sleepwalking or "mad" scene and the scene in which her body is carried away behind Macbeth. These patterns are recognized by the actors, and attentive audience members and critics have noticed them in other shows. My point is that if you put yourself in the audience's place, and you unfold the story in an interesting way that accentuates the storytelling that has been built into the show, then these kinds of patterns must underlie the behavioral lines and flows in the way that good composition underlines beautiful paintings. Designing and coding staging areas is an art, don't forget that. You need to place yourself in the audience and then create the flow that best helps to tell your story.

That you build this beauty into the experiential behavior as well as the performative behavior is what is so precious—it's an essential aspect of gorilla theatre, and a thread that stitches together the audience and the actors in many ways. This is happening during the performance, and the participation (I call it "collusion" in interviews) of the audience is a very pervasive energy. The movement massages them. In a way, there is a kind of rehabilitation in the treatment of a shared space as truly public. Preliminary audience-flow issues can be addressed simply by walking around the space and checking out sight lines, moves, and the frame that distance creates around a scene as it is being approached.

You can move the audience to a place that they can't see from where they are, but it needs to be timed well. You accomplish this by starting them out in one direction—say, toward the side of an obstacle. Then, as the first audience members get close, but not quite at front-row-seating proximity, you move the scene again. The rest of the audience has caught up enough to hear, and they understand that the move is twofold when they see and hear the second part of the move and see the lights change. If anything, a double shift when executed properly, helps to step up the audience's pace. Behavioral cues from the actors are a subtle but essential issue in analyzing audience flow during the transitions from scene-site to scene-site. It is the participation in the audience, experienced in your imagination, that helps reduce the desire to use too many scene areas. The audience needs to be encouraged to learn and to use the skill of moving with the show, and the show must teach each audience each night. This can encourage audience members to return, and to use their skill to experience new vantage points from which to view their favorite scenes and lines—or the entire performance.

chapter three

Establishing Corporate Culture

Observations

My theory is that every show is a corporation of its own. It follows, then, that it will have a corporate culture of its own as well. In fact, this idea is borne out by the style in which most for-profit production houses are organized. A producer will have an office and a small staff, but each individual show that the producer has originated will be incorporated separately—although the reins are still held pretty tightly from the main office. Each production is born, lives its own life, and eventually (or quickly) dies. The production organization as a separate entity goes on. I have seen a number of shows, during their lives, treated with a degree of recklessness regarding the values and ethics that are a part of any group endeavor, conscious or not. So, make yours a conscious effort. These values and ethical standards are key tools, as they form the basis for any independent decision making that might become necessary for your team members.

Remember: It is not during smooth sailing that a crew is really tested. The fibers that will hold your company together are woven from the very beginning of your efforts to organize and produce a gorilla-style production. And, as we all know from experience, even in the controlled environment of the theatre building, there are still variables to deal with during performance, and problems that need to be solved on the spot in order for the show to go on. Outdoors, or in a public place, the variables multiply, and your organization (cast, crew, and all) needs to be ready to handle the unknown and turn it into something entertaining.

And remember this: When external order breaks down, it is each team member's internalized understanding of order that will carry you through the moment. This concept, perhaps more than any other, should make it clear that the corporate culture, and the values instilled there, are as much a part of your organization and production as the costumes are.

If there is one idea that my experience of running things has taught me, it is this: Leave a position open rather than fill it with someone you don't believe in. The spot filled by someone who is far from your standard is going to be a drain on the whole team, and there will be no way to fix it short of radical surgery—firing them and finding a replacement—even when it is the right thing to do.

All of the productions that people have loved from the Gorilla Repertory Theatre Company since 1992 are success stories. And it seems as though every night something happens that makes it clear that we are all working from a shared set of values.

Responding to Conflicts

A good group will circle the wagons, so to speak, when there is a problem. One instance of a team coming together in a time of crisis has stuck with me.

A Midsummer Night's Dream was moving along well that night. It was the first or second performance of the year, and we had good crowds. Having moved to another part of Washington Square Park from where we had been for years, the audience had increased. So, it was opening weekend, and we had big crowds and lots of excitement as the show moved from place to place. But there were two hidden problems sneaking up on us.

One problem, the chief problem, was that I had grown complacent and had not drilled the idea of "cut." I might have mentioned it once, but I hadn't emphasized it as I usually had (and as I have done since). The other problem was a very powerfully built young man who had decided to take powerful drugs and wander around the city. By the time he wandered across our show in progress, he had become very violent. In fact, he punched and kicked audience members unprovoked, and eventually he broke a bottle with which to menace the crowd.

I was monitoring the situation and had called "cut." However, since the procedure hadn't been drilled well enough, the actors went back to work before I said "action." The assailant ran away from the crowd but over to a woman who happened to be passing by and hit her repeatedly. I ran over to help and found myself face-to-face with a very large, very angry person bent on doing harm to me. I responded by putting the heavy flashlight I was carrying across his head as quickly and as forcefully as I could manage in an attempt to stop him.

My calls for police assistance, which had been many during the incident, were finally heeded, and the police arrived. (This was before Mayor Giuliani had increased the number of police in New York City. Still, it wasn't the Wild West out there, and this has proven to be an isolated and unfortunate incident.) I was arrested for assault with a deadly weapon and taken to jail, where I spent forty-eight hours. The charges were dropped when the case came to trial, as my actions were so clearly in the defense of myself and others.

I tell you this story to show you how grateful I am to the cast and crew and to demonstrate, as I've mentioned, how well a team can come together in a time of crisis. They could have all gone home, they could have all freaked out, they could have all quit. They did none of these things. They kept track of me so that I never felt alone or abandoned; the stage manager took the names and phone numbers of hundreds of audience members who were willing to testify on my behalf as to what had happened; and they kept each other informed of developments in the situation. There was someone there when I was released in the middle of the night; there was someone there when I went to court a few months later. These are good people, and they shared specific values, not only in general but also about the gorilla-theatre work.

Success Story: *Macbeth* Actors Grab Flashlights

Another example of the team working together successfully occurred during the first year of the production of *Macbeth* at Fort Tryon Park, when the lighting rental company gave us equipment that was heavy and old. I had it tapped into a streetlight pole and a yard box (a circuit-breaker box), as usual. All would have been fine if it weren't for the fact that the dimmers hadn't been cleaned inside since 1950 or so.

As I remember, it was somewhere during the third weekend of the run. The review had come out in the *Times*, and so good crowds had swelled to amazing crowds and all was under way. During the heat of the climactic action, as Lady Macbeth was turning in a perfectly tuned performance, the dimmers blew. My thought was that the excess dust buildup had caught fire briefly on the copper brushes from a small spark. Yes, copper brushes—we were renting whatever equipment we could that year. At any rate, all the lights went off.

Before I could get to the nearby supply truck and grab the flashlights to hand to actors standing by, they already had them out and trained on Lady Macbeth—squatting in the front row, *Midsummer*-style—and they were holding the lights over the audience's heads in the back row of standees. That's the real spirit of the outdoor avant-garde. That is gorilla theatre. "Sweet are the uses of adversity," as they say. And on they went, scene to scene. Each scene was well lit, with reactive actors keeping the focus both literally and figuratively moving and handing off the lights to each other as needed.

I isolated the burned dimmer box and hot-patched the rest of the show on the two remaining boxes. It was not easy, and it was not elegant, but it was effective. Years later, I have taken to lighting *Macbeth* with an enhanced set of flashlights because I could see the "spooky" quality of them as the sun went down. The discipline of the actors helps make for a somewhat martial atmosphere, contributing mightily to the overall performance.

Are there "failure stories" too? Of course. In trying to expand the aesthetic, I have mistakenly brought people aboard who had no idea how or, more important, why this work is done. It isn't for people who think that it is a cheap alternative to indoor production. They just don't understand the aesthetic forces that are awakened by gorilla theatre, do not understand how strongly the audiences feel the truth of the work and how quickly. You know, if the work is boring and irrelevant, there's no amount of running around that is going to make it interesting. Our first *Richard III* proved that, unfortunately, by drawing out modern, proscenium scene relations strung haphazardly across a long, narrow stretch of park. The actors were given no coaching on the audience relationship, and three-quarters of the audience left during each performance. My production of *Pirates of Penzance*, staged on board the ship *Peking* at South Street Seaport, was so successful that my assistant and some staff stole the concept outright, attracted producers, and reopened it. They brought in huge amplifiers and smarmy gags, and increased the audience capacity at the expense of the gorilla-theatre movement that I had so carefully created. The pictures and diagrams that I had drawn up so specifically for the director assisting on that production must have been torn up and discarded. And, as you might guess, the resulting mess was a complete flop. There are other failures—I have had plenty. They have never been due to any problem with the popular gorilla-theatre aesthetic, but only my own failure to execute it properly. This book is specifically designed to serve the needs of those who want to build and serve a gorilla-theatre show. It takes a lot of heart, and you shouldn't do it for the wrong reasons.

Running Effective Meetings

Meetings of your work groups should be living systems. These work groups can be formed around different areas of responsibility, such as business and marketing, site relations, and so on. A production meeting consists of the producer, director, and all of the chief collaborating design staff. Of course, we've all seen people masquerading as directors who are really just committee heads, leading nothing and inspiring no one. Your central tasks are to lead and inspire and a good way of doing that is to run an efficient meeting. If production meetings are run efficiently, the production staff becomes aware that you value efficiency. This value becomes a key part of your show's corporate culture. It's one thing to talk about respecting your collaborators' time, but to do it is what earns you the respect that you need to lead well and inspire good work.

The basic model I use is, at its heart, parliamentary. Don't let that daunt you, because it works. First, it is imperative that you establish an agenda for the meeting, and put it in writing. This is a simple list of the areas that need to be reported on and the tasks that need to be completed or scheduled. The people attending the meeting should have been contacted in advance to solicit additions to the agenda, and they should all have a copy in advance.

Then, running the meeting is simple: You stick to the agenda. At the end, you talk about agenda items for the next meeting, and you review the "to-do's" that the meeting has generated.

An important feature of every production meeting should be a report from every section head, even if they are heading up a department of one. The stage manager is the perfect person to record what gets done at these meetings. Because the stage manager's primary purpose in production is to facilitate communication between departments, it makes sense to have the stage manager be in charge of the meeting's record. Ideally, this record should be posted where everyone can access it easily.

Always set a beginning and an end time for your meeting, and then stick to it. Let me repeat that: *Always set a beginning and an end time for your meeting, and then stick to it.* Of course, this will necessitate keeping an eye on the clock during the meeting. This is a wise idea in any event, and reminding team members, in a gentle and positive manner, that comments should be kept to the current topic and to the point will be helpful for keeping the tone of the meeting businesslike without being overly heavy.

If someone is late, start without him or her. If someone is late habitually, I suggest working without him or her. When a team member is late for a good reason, as happens from time to time, cover agenda topics for which they are not directly needed until they arrive. Ending a meeting before the scheduled stopping time is advisable, if the business has been completed. It will make team members more understanding if in the future an emergency demands a little more time than allotted, and, again, it shows a respect for the professional time of your collaborators.

The values you impart in team meetings will be tested in the field. The old business maxim that you should never make a decision until you must is nonsense in gorilla theatre. In a real way, your art is made up of decisions.

chapter **four**

Casting

Ideas and Ideals

In auditions, you will see a large number of actors, each for a brief amount of time. The general complaints about auditions are too numerous to go into here, but many of these complaints can be addressed by running your auditions efficiently. The "cattle call" style of audition is perceived as being the most disrespectful of actors, and this is with good reason. Whenever possible, actors should be given an exact audition appointment time, and this should be adhered to as zealously as possible. Your auditions are an opportunity not only to market your show to prospective cast members, but also to market your company to the acting community. I am very proud of how often my casting ability has been complimented, and this section is meant to explain the factors that I think contribute to my success in casting. I hope that this background will help your casting efforts.

For those uninitiated into gorilla-theatre-style performance, the perceptions of your company or project will vary. Clean, efficient, respectful auditions that thoroughly adhere to the guidelines set out in Actors' Equity materials will focus the actors' attention on the work and its demands. There's nothing wrong with having printed materials—your mission statement, bios of key members of your company or project, and reviews of your work—available for those who wish to educate themselves further on the form for which they are auditioning.

I find that using casting directors and managers can be one way to winnow down the crowd; in the end, however, the more actors you can see, the better. Discovering a talent ready to burst into this work is exciting, too. What is the spark that you are looking for? It is certainly not reducible to mere physical type, though you may have one in mind for a particular role. It is not reducible to physical grace and control, although, again, you may require this for your vision of a particular character. I don't think I need go into the harmful nature of simply combing résumés for content. Suffice it to say that it cheapens the work and it spoils something about the work's true quality early on. See the people and what they can do in two minutes—that's what they ask, and it is not much compared to the value of the ultimate result: a great cast.

You are observing the actors and gathering information about their working styles and so much more. No one exercise or policy is going to guarantee success, and you will learn what it takes in an actor to do this work as you do more gorilla-theatre productions. Casting is always key, nowhere more so than in a Shakespearean production. As Michael Feingold writes in his *Village Voice* pan of *Twelfth Night* at the Delacorte in 2002,

> Shakespeare's art is never rigid. Symmetry is always set off in two ways, by human individuality and by poetry. The three elements together, you might say, make up the music of the Shakespearean stage. . . . Writing for a permanent company, he tailored roles both to fit and to challenge artists whose abilities he knew. Burbage played all his leads, and Armin (at the time of *Twelfth Night*) all his clowns, but each hero or clown is a different person, and makes different demands on the actor. If you can't see the person, you are not seeing the play; and if the person you see doesn't match the text you hear, the director is at fault.

When I coach actors in audition technique, I often suggest that the most productive way to look at an audition is as two minutes to show what you love about the theatre. Performing! Here's a small audience of theatre lovers, however jaded, who are here to experience your work. I know that when I'm in the audition room, I look for actors who seem to love what they are doing even as they are doing it extremely well.

And remember that this audition will be the last chance you get to see this actor in a true performance until opening night. How are they handling it? Are they born to it? Do they make you feel assured, like they are comfortable and at home in the theatre, the performance environment? The answers to these questions contain information about how the actors will be making your audience feel, on a basic level. What is the atmosphere in the room like during their two-minute performance?

The old theatre saw says that the casting decision makers have already made their decision within the first three lines. For me, it's often the first three words, to be frank. And when those three words are what I'm looking for, it only makes the rest of the one hundred and fifteen seconds something to look forward to!

I love the theatre. In fact, I love it so much that I have found a wonderful way to bring it outside of the theatre building and put it into the hearts and minds of audience members wherever they are. I love it so much that I want to give the very best of it away to anyone who wants it, so much that I founded an aesthetic to reach beyond my own limited ability to do this, and sacrificed whenever necessary to fulfill this mission. For one thing, I have become a pretty good judge of people who, like me, have dedicated the majority of their time to working hard to optimize their theatrical talents. Think about it: Would you really want a doctor who hates what she does to operate on you? Should you enjoy the food of someone who hates to cook? Should you cast an actor who doesn't love the theatre?

Gorilla theatre is only gorilla theatre if it is good theatre first. Bad theatre spread out all over the landscape has proven time and time again to not be gorilla theatre. Good theatre needs good actors, and ninety percent of good directing is working with good actors. In auditions, you will see many, many people, and just about as many neuroses manifested. Do not make the stupid, jaded old theatre hack mistake of treating even the least talented and most neurotic person as anything less than a person. Remember: They are as capable of saying nice things about your work, your company, and the audition process as anyone else. So do what you need to do to feel calm and relaxed, confident, and mentally present and happy for the audition process. If you can't, wait until you are ready. It will be worth it, for the people you attract will be ready too, and you will be more equipped recognize them.

A final word on audition technique: I will sometimes ask an actor for permission to work with their monologue, to "sketch" as I call it. I ask them if I can direct it a little, just to see what happens. If the actor has seemed interesting and I sense the gorilla ability just below the surface, I will give notes to encourage a gorilla-style interpretation. Here are a few questions that I often use: Would you please pretend that there is an audience on all four sides of you and try to take beats to each pair of imaginary eyes that you see there? Would you let this influence the movement that you make? Could you try it imagining that you are acting through your back, too? Would you mind doing it again, this time pretending that this little room is a big, wide-open space (Here you would look for the actor's sense of presence, not sheer volume.) Would you do it again, moving around a lot, even moving in a way different from the character's way of moving? You'd be surprised at how often something that feels to an actor as "not how the character would move" turns out to be a really interesting way for the character to move. Actors are subjected to a lot of bad acting teachers who give them negative reinforcement and make them lock up physically with fear. Sometimes laughter is the best medicine. Hey, it's a gorilla-style show, could you run around and do the monologue as if the character had been turned into a monkey? Amo Gulinello's monkey-style acting is a thing of sheer beauty, and you'd cast him after seeing it once, I believe. I think I did, as a matter of fact!

Respect for Actors and Demands of the Form

Physical stamina is an important part of gorilla theatre. The breath, strength, and muscle tone needed for this style of performance are not to be underestimated. When asked for a short answer about what it takes to be a good gorilla actor, I'll often respond this way: Run as fast as you can for two hundred yards, then deliver a Shakespearean monologue brilliantly, with animation, enthusiasm, characterization, presence, and power. Actors who make their performance seem effortless are my ideal.

Jy Murphy's work with Gorilla Rep is probably my acme for this aspect of the work. It started with his audition—the Launce monologue where he is complaining about his dog. I was in stitches as Jy seemed to teleport himself here and there around the room, reflecting on his imaginary dog—which I could see clearly—and his comic moments were punctuated with physical suspensions that were like instant freeze-frames. As we spoke afterward, I realized that he had exerted himself tremendously to create this performance, yet it had seemed effortless. Jy Murphy went on to bounce Oberon, Ubu, Petruchio, and others off the walls of Judson Church and back at our Washington Square Park crowds with clear, supported vocal energy.

The long answer is that I have a huge amount of respect for the physical effort that it takes to do this work. I've had actors who were "overweight" by current standards do as well as any others—they were strong and able. Let's face it: Falstaff is fat! Why not? Let the movies cast people who have no talent and stereotypical bodies and faces—the gorilla theatre is alive with

Eric K. Daniels (center, in hat) as the Governor of Harfleur in Gorilla Rep's *Henry V* in Northampton, Massachusetts, 2002. Here, the audience plays the residents of the besieged town as the governor steps into their midst on the bench. He and the audience face King Henry and Exeter on the rock. Photo by Mark Schneider.

talent. Sexy people come in all shapes and sizes, and so do good gorillas. What is essential is the physical ability to handle the kind of exertion that a good gorilla show needs. Richard Boleslavsky notes in *Acting: The First Six Lessons* that undertaking physical culture is a very basic and early step for any actor to take. Tad Carducci performs line after line of Puck's dialogue completely upside down in a handstand, and the audiences love it!

Different types of physical training have resulted in actors' increased abilties, and, like technique, training is an individual thing. Yoga, marathon training, Pilates, various martial arts, and just plain gym and aerobic workouts have all seemed to work well for various people. Allan Wayne's training regiment seems about ideal, if there is an ideal, and I know that the contact improvisation and six-viewpoints work that I did helped me as a performer. I suppose swing dancing would do just as well for the right actor. The will and drive that it takes to keep going after you are tired adds real strength to the work that is deeper than mere physical strength, and it helps carry a gorilla show from place to place as it goes from scene to scene.

As an exmaple, in July 2002, we put together four full run-throughs of *Henry V*, one of them a paratheatric rehearsal run, as well as a line-through, all in one day, and all four of the runs were outdoors. We also did gesture work (see chapter 6) that day, and other exercises. The next day we performed the show in Northampton to great success. I never insisted on any of this; I simply asked the cast if they were ready to handle the next task. They had the physical and mental stamina to make this all work well for the show. It was an intensified period of work, and it really lit up the performance. Our audience was amazed that only six actors were on the grass for the curtain call—they had thought it was more like eighteen! I can't adequately describe the speed of the costume changes and, more important, the character changes, that this production required. It was a push, and a new kind of gorilla-theatre show, and the cast had the basic energy and stamina that the show demanded in order to be great.

Enthusiasm for the Form

It may not be necessary for people who understand the form to work well in it, but it sure helps. Mental acuity is hard to judge in an audition situation, but simply asking a few questions can give you an idea of an actor's ability to think on his feet. If the actor would rather be anywhere else than right here in front of this audience right now, he or she is not really an actor. Longing for imaginary stages is no substitute for enthusiasm about the stage that is set and ready to perform.

If you are working with actors who are early in their careers, they might not have realized that all the real pros have paid their dues in myriad forms of theatre as their careers progressed. Maybe we all need a certain quota of applause and appreciation to counteract the negative reinforcement that society doles out so readily to theatre artists—especially experimental ones. Once this quota is reached, we can move confidently in the art form and in the world. And so we get that quota in lofts and summer-stock companies, in basements and Off-Off-Broadway nooks and crannies.

At the end of the day, actors who are excited about gorilla theatre and all of its potential are going to be an inspiration to have around. Their attitude will have only as much impact on the other actors as they are a force in the work. The better they do, the more they will be listened to, and this is to the production's benefit. If an actor wants to get back to the real heart of the art form, I believe it is possible with gorilla theatre. I've seen it happen in parks all over the place. The more mercenary and grasping the actor is, the more difficult it is for him or her to see how important it is that the audience is experiencing theatre in a whole new way. When an actor's entire existence is centered around the sentence "Hi, can you get me cast in a commercial?" you have to wonder about their reasons for doing this work. Strictly speaking, gorilla theatre is exciting and dynamic and can be as good a place as any for a casting agent to find an actor. It is the actors' responsibility to fit the work into their career plan, not ours.

The only way to fit into the career plans of great actors is to pursue your own goals, and to make these goals as clear as you can to the actors you are auditioning. I have always found it beneficial to remember that if I can't get the right team together it is best to wait until I can, even if that means canceling a show. Fortunately, this has happened very rarely. A large part of this success has come from seeing many actors and holding out for the ones who are not only talented but also right for the aesthetic and the particular show. It can be hard to be around so many people who want you to do something—hire an actor, call an end to the audition process—even if it is the wrong thing for your show. It takes a certain toughness of mind. However, seeing a great actor who is clearly full of the kind of energy that we need in the parks for gorilla theatre will bring a smile to the toughest face. I have had to tell actors from time to time that I am impressed with their work but don't have a role for them in this particular project. They don't believe me, of course, but when I call them back for other projects and do cast them eventually, they change their tune. The right stuff doesn't change easily, even in the face of disappointment.

Character Basics and Physical Motion

The ability to move in and out of character instantly, even in the most demanding of situations, is an important one in gorilla theatre. The actor who can give an interesting performance of *Richard III* only after brooding, wandering around for hours "in character," and annoying a stagehand or two is decidedly not a gorilla-theatre actor. If you are suspicious in auditions that an actor might behave this way, it is possible sometimes to find out if they have the gorilla ability or, perhaps, allow them to discover it in themselves instantly. As the actor is running through the monologue a second time, having warned them this was coming, of course, say, "Freeze!" forcefully. Then, after a brief pause, "Action!" The seamlessness that you see here is good information, as is the actor's willingness to try a few simple games or sketches. No one exercise is the make or break in an audition or callback, and you need to be gathering information with this in mind at all times.

This kind of thing makes some people angry, and in an audition situation that is bound to happen from time to time. It is natural. You just have to find actors who have some mental toughness, a sense of humor, and the ability to turn seeming adversity to their advantage in performance. You like an actor who addresses a line or two to a person who happens to walk into the wrong studio while they are in the middle of their monologue. That indefinable feeling that a character is present is so important. I often feel as if this character is painted on a canvas of enthusiastic sincerity, but if it is, it is painted with the brush of an able physicality. What I am trying to get at, but explaining poorly, is a link between enthusiasm and the physicality required to transfer that enthusiasm to an audience that I have percieved over many successful gorilla productions.

In asking an actor to move around the room more as they work, you look for the most basic character dimensionality. Does the character walk, or does the actor walk around talking? Also, a practical sense of scale is a real asset in an actor. It can be communicated through direction, of course, but it is something to investigate in an actor. Josh Spafford gave a great example when he auditioned for me for the first time. His "St. Crispin's Day" speech from *Henry V* was entertaining, flawless, interesting, well nuanced and shaded . . . just extraordinary. And it was intimate. The scaling was perfect for the room and for the three of us watching. I complimented the work and asked him to imagine that the room was a football field and the officers he was addressing were in the stands. It is a common mistake to make with this speech—it is not an address to the troops in the style of General Patton but a rallying of the officers and leaders who will, in turn, go into the field and lead the troops. If Henry can sell his officers on the battle ahead, they will win the army for him, and that is the only way to win the day against the terrible odds he is facing. So, with this in mind, and the scale I was asking for, the actor took the energy through the roof—really shook the walls—without forgetting the situation that the character is in, and with a fully shaded performance.

Working in Further Detail

Once you have a sketch going with an actor, if you have time it is good to work on a few detailed notes. Particular lines and beats—not too many—should be pointed out and worked over a bit. My casting technique feels easy when it works correctly. At the end of the session, I simply think back on which people I have already started working with in the audition, and I cast them. When I say *working*, I mean specifically working on the show.

For example, Sean Seibert thought his chances were best of being cast as Demetrius in *A Midsummer Night's Dream* the first time he auditioned for me. He had played the role before, and our rehearsal was to be a short one. I didn't realize this, of course, as I hadn't glanced at his résumé (as usual). We worked on his monologue and were able to go from the basic sketch into some detail work on the monologue. It was, as I recall, not even a comic monologue, but the energy and the detail were clear; as I looked back on the work, I realized that I had been thinking of him as Bottom ever since the audition. I didn't need to call him back—he was cast and did a brilliant job on that and other subsequent Gorilla Rep shows.

I have been trusting my instincts for years, and I believe that has taught them to be clear. Working in toward the detail is a technique that takes patience, but I believe it does improve your instincts. An old story that some colleagues tell about me is true; I did slip and say "Hi, Puck—er, I mean—Ken, did you say you name was?" when I met actor Ken Schatz for the first time. I guess it was a little odd, until Ken went out and did an amazing job with the role. As he'll confirm, I put him through extra paces in the detail department to confirm my hunch.

The ability to work in further details is one that lets me understand and learn a lot about an actor's work. It may account for the fact that I often cast an actor in a role without having read them in it. I'll discuss this further in the section on callback practices, but I want to say that looking at an actor as something more than a cog in a predictable machine is important. Even in the tightest three-minute time slot, you can see a two-minute monologue and have a chance to work with an actor a bit if you choose to. What I always do force myself to do is observe each actor's monologue in its entirety. If it is not working for me, it is at the very least an opportunity to think over how I might approach teaching them if that were my job. Once, after one of the worst monologues that I have ever forced myself to sit through, the actor turned to me at the end with the most unbelievable grin on his face and thanked me. He said that it was the first time anyone had let him finish the monologue in an audition. I've seen him in the audience from time to time. He does love the theatre, and so do I. But in the end, I would not be doing anyone a favor by casting him in a demanding role that he was not ready for.

Techniques and Scheduling

Startling things happen in a gorilla-theatre performance, often wonderfully startling things. I have found that casting people who—in addition to being talented, knowing some technique, and having great discipline and a strong work ethic—have the ability and confidence needed to include a bit of the unexpected is a great idea. I came upon one idea quite by accident, and by accident I found out how well it works. There was a time when I was behind schedule for one reason or another. The actor presenting a monologue was clear and energized, used the existing audience well, and moved well, and my instinct was that he was a perfect candidate for the role. I knew all of this two or three lines into the monologue, so I burst up from my seat saying, "Great! We'll see you at callbacks." I shook his hand, I meant what I said, I saw him at callbacks, and I was glad that I did. Since then, I have sometimes tried this technique when I was unsure about the actor's basic aplomb or ability to handle the unexpected. Can you believe that some actors find this insulting? Only when their cool is a facade, of course. The few times I went ahead and cast such folks, they never found a way to look at the demands of the performance and the oddities of the site as gifts to be played with. Maybe I'm nuts—it worked this way sometimes.

When I schedule auditions, I am so focused on adding to the value of the actors' experience that I sometimes forget to take care of myself as well. Scheduling regular breaks improves my overall performance. I try to take at least twenty minutes every three hours or so to reflect and allow the actors' work to settle in. This is not a time for shuffling head shots, but a real breather. Time to think. When feasible, I take these breaks in the audition room and ask my staff to take a break too, to talk to the actors as they come in, to get a cup of coffee, or whatever. I like the quiet that settles into the room after all of the motion and fullness of the work. It is an example of actively cultivating the subconscious; an "atmosphere," as Michael Chekhov might call it, arrives for me, and I know it is helpful to the process.

Russell Marcel as Banquo's ghost in *Macbeth* at Fort Tryon Park, New York City, June 2000. Photo by Benjamin Heller.

Actors' Equity requires that a monitor be present in the room when you audition an actor, and I think that this is a good practice. From time to time, I have been left without a stage manager to monitor some period of the audition. When this happens, I have found it helpful to bring the actors into the audition room two at a time. One monitors the other, then they switch. It is an experience similar to being a "reader," who plays opposite candidates in a casting call. I find that it works well. One of my favorite audition calls was somewhat strange. During the casting of *Faust: The New Musical Comedy*, Chris Barron and I were faced with a bit of a difficulty. We couldn't audition people in a nice facility, because I had put all of the project's budget elsewhere, and the budget was on the lean side at that. So we found ourselves auditioning in a run-down old former school building euphemistically called a "cultural center." It had occasionally been a court of last resort, and I thought weekend auditions in the daytime would go fine. The professional musical theatre crowd saw things differently: they looked decidedly uncomfortable in the mismatched chairs lined up in rows down the hallway outside our little schoolroom. Chris is well known, of course, and the project was to be very successful in Grand Central Terminal, but at the time our colleagues looked less than enthused. Chris and I put our heads together—he's such a consummate performer that the audience outside needing comfort and cheer was a natural draw. So we popped outside the audition room and sang a comic duet from the show. As the crowd turned over and new troops of fresh faces fell at the sight of our dusty, run-down digs, we would head back out and do another funny little ditty from the show. Singing "Ketchup with a Flair" really did bring smiles to their faces, and we ended up with a good experience for all and a great cast to boot.

Now, in gorilla theatre, a setback is often an opportunity to shine. I was auditioning for *Macbeth* one year when we got booted out of our rehearsal space on Eighth Avenue earlier than expected. We had one more actor show up, and he struck me as a nice guy. After a bit of a chat, with grins on our faces, we reached the conclusion that, since it was to be a gorilla show, maybe he should audition right there on the street! He handled the situation with aplomb. Strolling at ease back and forth in front of the building, he turned it into a real gorilla performance. Fortunately, we had stage management there—myself, two stage managers, and at least one other actor. We were an attentive audience there on the street, and he even managed to attract a few passersby! We all applauded as he finished, the folks strolled on with smiles on their faces, and we had cast a brilliant actor as Banquo!

Callback Practices and Forms

GROUP IMPROVISATIONS: IMPULSE CIRCLE

The Impulse Circle is a useful technique in rehearsal. There, the actor needs to be focused on the character, or characters, and on the story being told. In a callback, a wider kind of work can occur, and it can get very interesting. There are numerous variations on this basic acting game—here's mine in a nutshell. First, the actors stand in a circle. For spacing purposes, it is sometimes best to ask them to start by standing shoulder to shoulder, then take a step back, then another, and so on until they are in a neat circle in the space, with room to move.

Then you explain the idea of "neutral" to the actors. We'll go into this in more detail in the chapter on rehearsal techniques, but essentially, neutral means arms released and relaxed, feet shoulder-width apart and parallel, and with the actors' attention focused through their peripheral vision on the two actors on either side of them.

You ask the actors to create a short, repeatable, full-body and full-voice gesture. This is aimed at the actor on one side of them, and it passes around the circle in that direction. It keeps going in the same direction until you clap loudly (a few times in rapid succession), at which time the impulse can pass through, or be sent right back. It is imperative to go back to neutral after the gesture is completed, no matter how many times it gets mirrored instead of passed. This makes the true, basic conflict clearer, and it makes for an intensifying and organic change—not an artificial "interesting choice." The less clichéd the gesture is, the more filled with meaning it is for the partner (an analog for the audience in some ways, and also for scene partners). A second series of claps can signal the ability to pass the gesture across the circle as well, but this gets into a level of concentration more in concert with rehearsal intensity. You get to see actors work with each other very quickly here, and the amount of self-confidence it takes to get up in a stranger's face and really *gesture* is probably roughly equivalent how much it takes to get in front of an audience and really *act*.

You can also add mirroring and other basic gesture-generation techniques to your callbacks to observe these kinds of generations and reactions.

Instant Characters

The "instant character" game works well in callbacks when you can fit it in—especially if you are casting a comedy. Comedy is difficult, and not everyone is comfortable with people laughing at them. It's a skill in itself. Instant character starts with the actors, preferably fewer than fifteen, standing in a line, all facing the same direction, shoulder to shoulder. Next, the first actor in line walks to stand facing the line in the center of the space. The second actor in line quickly moves to stand next to the first, and creates a physical suspension—like a pose, and preferably not a clichéd one. You can explain to the actors that you are looking for originality, or leave it to them—observing which actors' instinct takes them away from the dreaded "look-I'm-drinking" pose. The first actor duplicates this pose. The second actor returns to the line after checking over the first actor once to see if there is a glaring difference. The third actor then makes a vocal sound from the line, something verbal but not a word—a vocal texture, a sound, a warble, a groan, any sound. The first actor, in position now, imitates the vocal sound. The fourth actor calls out a word to the first actor, who delivers the word using the vocal quality that he or she is already duplicating. With these three elements—pose, vocal texture, and word—a character occurs instantly in the perception of the audience. The actor gets a few seconds to move the character around, explore the character's mode of locomotion. If it is flat, or it doesn't seem to be coming alive, you should start over and let the second, third, and fourth actors try inputting new choices. When the character appears, though, and walks around for a moment, you say "done" clearly, the actor goes to opposite end of the line from which he or she started, and everyone moves down one place. This is repeated until all of the actors have created an instant character.

Next, the actors are put into groups of two or three to try a brief improvisational scene. Sculpting a beginning, middle, and an end to a brief scene can be aided by calling "cut" yourself, or by allowing the actors to cut off the scene themselves. A final stage can be added that has the whole room full of characters, moving around and creating a more complex scene. Observe the actors' reaction to this, as it is related to the rehearsal practices you will learn about in chapter 5. As with all improvisations, but specifically in callbacks, you are looking for the ability and talent expressed but also for the adaptability and ease that the actor exhibits. Who among these candidates is going to help you build a strong team?

It is a good idea to do a dry-run demonstration or walk-through of the exercise with part of your team before you embark on it with auditioners.

chapter **five**

Rehearsal Techniques

Introduction: Use What You Know

The work you have done on interior theatrical productions will serve you well in your preparations for a gorilla show. That body of experience will have shown you what it feels like when an audience reacts to your work in an engaged and strong way. We want to multiply that effect on your peripatetic outdoor audiences. Every cue, every sign, every possible way to communicate to them must be explored and enveloped. The details are just as important as they are in any theatre building—there are just many more of them, and they diffuse and flow through your audience in different ways.

One simple example is actor focus. There is no "offstage" in the park. As an actor prepares, or even just waits for an entrance, his or her total focus and concentration on the action that is occurring will focus the audience's attention more sharply than any spotlight. Collapsing into an "internal" preparation method (this should be accomplished farther away from the main action than the standby area) will create a distracting miniperformance that will leave a few audience members confused. You haven't been instructing the audience with the internal cues of your staging to be passive voyeurs. Rather, you and your actors have been leading them into an active state of correct participation. So what will audience members do when they look to the side area and see one very intense actor focusing hard on the action in the current stage area? They'll look there, straight back to the action, to make sure that they don't miss anything that is so important that this actor is burning holes in it with the fire in her eyes.

There are many exercises to hone and sharpen actor focus. I'm sure you know many already, and with a little experimentation and augmentation they will do just fine in rehearsing for a gorilla-theatre production. There is an element of focus, of course, in everything that actors do, and in every exercise.

In addition to the classic mirror exercise, I like to do what I call the "blind exercise." In its basic form, the blind exercise is one actor leading another one around the room. The one who is following has his or her eyes closed. This can be done with a whole group of actors in pairs, or by one pair at a time. The leader should attempt to "show" the room to the follower, and for this reason it is often useful to rearrange the furniture and objects in the room. The trust that it takes to lead and to be led can form the basis for a variety of stage relationships, but even in its basic form it is a good exercise for building actor focus.

I'll give you an example of a variation that I built to bring this focused quality into an onstage relationship. During early rehearsal for a production of *Macbeth* at Fort Tryon Park, I was rehearsing in a room that had a mass of clutter along the wall. Old filing cabinets, dangerous-looking broken packing crates, and such were stacked around. I asked the actor playing Macbeth to stand in the center of the space and close his eyes. Then, I asked the three witches to drag the clutter out and around the open part of the space as loudly as possible. As they did so, you could see the change register on Macbeth's face.

Then, we simply did the blind exercise, with all three witches helping lead Macbeth around, alternating which of the three was the overall leader, choosing the direction, and so on. We sent one of the witches to scoot some clutter around for effect, and the three of them took very close care of Macbeth. Then, to complete Macbeth's experience of this link between focus and storytelling about the supernatural, the three of them placed him again in the center of the space, where he had started. One of them plugged his ears while the other two put all of the junk back into place, leaving the space empty again. Macbeth opened his eyes, and the landscape that he had experienced in the heightened state of sightlessness was gone! The actor came away from the exercise with a whole new feeling about the witches.

How Do You See?

In rehearsal, again and again, place yourself in the audience on opening night. What are they expecting? The actor's task is to stay completely rooted in the moment, right there in rehearsal. But part of your task as a

Marla Stolar as First Fairy becomes friendly with the audience. Photo by Lynda Kennedy.

director is to constantly contextualize what's going on in rehearsal and what it will mean in performance. You are balancing the creative work of the actor in that moment against the needs of the audience to understand the story and to participate in the world of the gorilla-theatre production. I really believe that it is possible in all phases of the rehearsal process to find things that will carry over well into performance. At every point, it is important to communicate the relative degree of polish that you are looking for from the actors. However, you shouldn't let this limit your inclusion of moments or ideas that come up. The freest improvisation will often yield directions and even specific moments that you will want to remember and include in your performance notes. Actors never mind hearing a note about a specific choice they made followed by the phrase "please keep that!"

Respect for the Audience

Because the theatre, as I have said, is built again every night, in every performance, out of the basic elements of the cast and the audience, it is vitally important to understand the audience's role at every level of a gorilla production. For the actors, this role is again and again one of inclusion in the action and in their characters' lives.

From the first steps implied in directions such as "the audience is always on your side" and "you are responsible for telling the story clearly," to more specific ones such as "the audience is the rest of the court here" or (for a monologue) "the audience is you in the mirror as you speak to yourself," the signs and signals are built up for our collaborators, the audience.

We gently—and sometimes urgently—point the audience in the direction of the emotional life, relationships, story, stakes, and holographic worldview of our performance. As with the most basic fact of audience flow, which I will address later, we are the ones to jump into the open arms of the audience, metaphorically. They always have the choice to move in and out of a more or less passive, observant state and into a direct emotional link with the play throughout our work on its performance.

As the scenes move from place to place, audience members make aesthetic choices that impact their own experience as well as the experience of other audience members. This is unusual, and has challenged critics to try to find a word for it. Because "audience participation" has already been used to refer to such effects as letting the audience decide the ending of a play, the term *gorilla theatre* will have to do.

Respect for the Text

The story that we tell is mapped out by the text, and everything is shaped in order to tell the story of the text clearly. We have had a lot of success staging Shakespeare in the gorilla style, but he is by no means the exclusive source of our success. W. B. Yeats and contemporary adaptations of classic literature and plays have worked well. There will be a time when brilliant playwrights create important contemporary work for the gorilla style.

To date, the contemporary works that have been submitted to me have been, for the most part, bad plays that the playwrights couldn't get produced indoors. En Garde Arts created a few gorilla-style staging plans for new works, but they were rare, and they had the problem of attaching a traditional box office to every show they put together. I would suggest looking for a playwright who has at least a few successful productions under his or her belt, who is excited by a gorilla-style show, and who launches into writing one with passion and a specific vision.

The play is something that you need to feel strongly about setting into the gorilla style, and during rehearsals you should make your enthusiasm for the text known to the actors and everyone else involved in the production. Each play that is of merit may, theoretically, have a perfect gorilla-theatre incarnation. We are still beginning our exploration of the style, so the play should be one that is motivating you very deeply to articulate it in this form. This will attract better and bigger audiences, and that always brings new resources to work with for the aesthetic as a whole.

The Character Meeting: Establishing Individual Communication

The character meeting has become an integral part of my work in gorilla theatre. Because the aesthetic has particular demands, as will the concept behind the production, it is important to begin to communicate these in terms of each actor's own techniques and experience. It is first necessary to get an idea of what these are. The character meeting is with individual actors, and usually lasts about thirty minutes. I spend most of the initial character meeting listening. The questions I ask include the following:

1. What is your training?
2. How do you usually approach a role?
3. What have you thought about this one?
4. Have you seen a gorilla-theatre-style show? (A good question to ask at callbacks, but, asked again here, it can serve as a jumping-off place for a discussion about the show.)
5. What is your homework like?
6. How early are you usually off book, and how do you get there?
7. What questions do you have for me?

Listen well, and take good notes as the gorilla actors speak about their work. You will understand their creation in rehearsal much better when you have some idea of their background and what they do for homework, and the insight into the character is valuable in shaping the show. A few gentle suggestions, usually in the form of questions, can be helpful if you sense a self-defeating or counterproductive line of reasoning or character construction.

This remains true throughout the rehearsal process. Character meetings can be requested by you or the actor, and some actors really benefit from almost weekly sessions to review and discuss the character work.

Although I generally discourage these meetings from being anything but face-to-face, distance and schedules being what they are, an e-mail on a particular focused question is sometimes necessary. The rule here is to keep the question and answer focused on a specific issue that needs to be addressed before proceeding. Following is one exchange that I have the actor's permission to quote for you, and my answer, to more clearly demonstrate the technique. To set up the scene, the actor is playing the Duke in *Othello*. He has given a wonderfully layered performance at the previous evening's rehearsal. It was of the scene in which the Duke is awakened late at night by two crises: the military crisis of the State, and Brabantio's crisis of his missing daughter, who has run off to marry Othello. The actor has darted his focus around the room, moving rapidly and giving a fairly stirring idea of a leader torn by various forces coming together in his "ready room" or "war room," as we might say. A leader we understood perfectly had been pulled out of his bed. The blocking had picked up specific patterns for the motion in the scene, and the formal placement, although dynamic and fast, was woven to help tell the overall story. This was the actor's question, and my response:

> ACTOR: What I have in mind might explain some of what I suspect looked like my uneasiness (mine, not the Duke's) in much of the scene. When Brabantio enters and presents me with a new crisis (or a complication, rather, in the crisis already at hand), the scene soon changes from a series of brief exchanges to a series of relatively lengthy discourses. The continuation of rapid pacing on the part of the Senators makes sense to me—their impatience with the Brabantio problem is consistent with this behavior. But *I* [The Duke] need to listen. Moreover, I need to listen relatively patiently (if I were THAT impatient, I'd interrupt those long-ass speeches) and to speak in a manner intended to calm down Brabantio. So, during rehearsal, I was trying, at the same time, to do things that felt inconsistent with each other: to move with a sense of urgency on the one hand, and to listen patiently and respond reassuringly on the other. It seems to me that I flipped back and forth between the two and was never really committed to either. I just thought you might want to know why, today, I had trouble following your direction.

> CHRISTOPHER: What I thought I saw was you handling the direction pretty well; the Duke does have to be a bit torn between the current crisis of the State and the personal crisis of Brabantio, a relatively highly placed

political and social figure as well as someone that you know and I think actually care for. So, the trick would be to commit to both and let the feelings flow from there, back and forth. The inconsistency is beautiful. Not to be harsh, but making one choice for a scene can often come across much like playing one note for an entire movement of a symphony. Even the most radical-seeming contradictions still lie within the precisely built snowflake-like multiangular matrix of your subconscious construct of the character. You can rely on me to guide you away from the appearance of unsupported character contradictions as well, even should such an anomaly crop up.

Scheduling Rehearsal

Usually, you will want to conduct the character meetings with the actors during the first few weeks after you have cast the show, when the first production meetings are occurring and when the stage manager is planning the schedule for the rehearsal process. I suggest giving the stage manager a detailed account of how much time you would like to have with each of the three phases of rehearsal—improvisation, work-through, and staging.

The way I establish this "wish list" of times is to go through and think it out scene by scene. Then I add up the hours and compare them to the total available in the rehearsal space. Usually I have overshot my resources, so I then calculate the percentage that each scene and phase needs to shed and pull that percentage off of each estimate, rounding down in most cases.

This saves me a little extra time to make sure that I am not pulling a scene rehearsal down below a half hour, which I have found to be the minimum for getting anything meaningful done. It is then up to the stage manager to juggle the actors' conflicts into the schedule, with the one caveat that the cast must move through each phase of the process for the complete play before moving on, if at all possible. Certainly, the order cannot be confused for the individual scenes.

A quick note about monologues: when you schedule time for rehearsal, it is also good to set aside time for monologue work with individual actors. I find that this fits in best near the end of the work-through process, as the structural needs of the monologues get clearer. It is also most productive to have the actor fully off book for monologue work, even if you need to set aside the text for improvisation work. Also, as the character meetings continue, if a need arises for one with an actor who has monologues, scheduling the character meetings and monologue rehearsals together can be very productive. It often happens that character issues are highlighted in the monologues, and clarifying these as they come up before putting them directly to work can be quite helpful.

The read-through is a good place to start, at the initial cast meeting. I have found that reading through the play with the actors on their feet helps set the tone for the work to come. There are many ways to accomplish this. I have settled on two forms that seem to serve me well most often, especially with Shakespeare.

In one form, the actors are seated in a circle. When they are reading a scene, they are asked to step into the circle. Movement with the book in hand can be dangerous, but it helps to have all of the actors in a scene up together. The merest glances of eye contact, a step or two toward or away from another character, can begin to sketch the underlying relationships in the scene.

In the other, even more dynamic form, the actors move in the grid formation, always at right angles, choosing to move at a fast, medium, or slow pace, and changing directions often. When reading, they are encouraged to stop and move only slowly and safely. This form puts an additional charge to the actors who are not "in" the scene being read at any given moment. This works when they get into the spirit of creating an atmosphere around the scene that is being read, and when they use it as an opportunity to listen actively. There is material in the entire text to draw from in improvisation, and it is worth noting that when describing the form to the actors.

In both forms, I encourage the actors to request clarification on word pronunciation or meaning. The spirit of the storytelling comes through, I find, when the actors are encouraged to commit to initial choices and have as much fun with the forms as possible. Which form to choose, or the decision to go with another form, is perhaps as much an aesthetic choice as anything. But it is worth noting that by getting the play in some kind of motion, even very early, an energized feeling can be imparted to the work. It is an early sample of, or a first step toward, the kind of intense energy, focus, and listening that make outdoor environmental acting work come alive.

The Three-Phase Technique: Improvisation, Work-Through, and Staging

This plan divides the rehearsal process into three phases: improvisation, work-through, and staging. Gorilla Rep rehearsals for a given production are a variation on this general plan, and I expect you to tailor it to the needs of your vision and specific production solutions.

The demands of improvisation on your cast are that they use it to work toward the inner landscape of the show and that they keep their eyes open for opportunities to help each other explore. Each technique and exercise will yield different results for each actor. When actors are struggling to find a way into an improvisation, it often helps for you to take them aside and make sure they understand the parameters of the work. Then, gently remind them that the other members of the cast may be making discoveries that will impact the production and that this process will help mold the show. Then, simply ask them to work for these other actors if they find themselves coming up dry in the improvisational work.

Work-through rehearsals are basically about running through scenes off book, but without having any specific blocking set. Often, the stage manager is still on book at this point, so actors can call for a line if need be. The work-through phase is about funneling the energy and the emotional discoveries into the specific demands of the text. As it progresses, you should see the need for specific blocking, but it is best to hold off on this until the staging begins. A few broad strokes or "traffic cop" directions to keep the story clear from your point of view and to keep the actors physically safe are not out of line, of course.

Staging rehearsal is all about exact physical motions and, to an extent, the targeting of line delivery. I ask that the actors note the staging completely in their scenes, to the degree that another actor could ask when and where they make a cross and they could answer. It is an exacting process but one that delivers results when handled correctly. Once a cast has mastered the specific blocking and stage movement, they will by necessity vary from it in a gorilla-style production.

Exact staging functions, as I sometimes say, like a jazz score. When an actor decides to stray from it, all of the others on stage know where he is heading and can join back in when he hits the expected marks, compensating as the story develops during the variation. Also, it is worth expressing to the cast as you begin staging that much of it will feel familiar to them—the improvisation process is a good time to start noting patterns and actions that can fit into the staging later. As these are brought back, often straightened out visually and crafted for timing by you, the actors will remember the improvisations that generated them. This will help the actors integrate them into the overall plan, and to recall the internal work that made them free inside the world of the production in the first place.

In the improvisation phase, a rhythm becomes established between flights of creative exploration and checking back in with the text for new areas to explore. This can be handled in a variety of ways, but I try to be straightforward about moving back and forth between the two as I feel the need arise.

There are many improvisational forms, of course, and description of them already fill many books. Certainly, almost any form can be adapted or used at the proper time; gorilla theatre is still theatre, of course. Here I intend to outline the forms that I use most often and almost invariably start out with.

This physical, gestural work has its roots in Jerzy Grotowski's early work with the Polish Theatre Lab, but those who shaped it also clearly learned and borrowed from other techniques. Included among these are the actor training methods of Sanford Meisner. The Iowa Theatre Lab carried the work forward most recently, and my basic rehearsal improvisation methods are closely modeled on those of Kevin Kuhlke at New York University's Experimental Theatre Wing. Bertolt Brecht's in there somewhere too, but I'll leave further academic-style genealogical analysis out of this practical explanation.

Gesture: Definition

For our purposes, a "gesture" is made up of a short, repeatable physical action accompanied by a vocal expression. The gesture should evoke motion in the spine ("full body," as I sometimes say) as well as in the vocal chords ("full voice"). Gestures are Short, Repeatable, Full Body, and Full Voice.

Furthermore, the gesture emanates from and returns to a neutral state in which the actor, fully aware and ready, is standing with feet placed in a parallel position at shoulder width, arms released and relaxed, spine and attention active, and peripheral vision engaged. Neutral in this sense is a highly useful state for an actor to return to at many points in the rehearsal process. It can provide a continuum between different improvisation forms, or an active space to add direction to a form from the outside, immediately continuing the work without the drop in energy that can come from a full stop or break. Neutral state makes it possible to fit together the necessary elements of the process without dropping the intensity of the work and starting from scratch.

The gesture has another crucial aspect as well. It must not be a cliché. Clichés can be interesting or funny but only once. A cliché or overly obvious everyday gesture can reduce the possibilities of the work, while an original gesture provides endless variations for interpretation. I have come to believe that the true gesture defines "abstract" in the clearest manner possible for a physical actor. The word *abstract* is far too often mistakenly defined in art as "meaningless." This is patently untrue in the gestural work, even exactly opposed to the truth of the matter.

In art, abstract means "evocative of subjective meaning" or "provocative of individual interpretation." Both ideas are far from the notions of "meaningless" or "empty." The original abstract gesture of a skilled actor will be overflowing with meaning and invested with the intensity that the effort brings. It's not about being overblown or beyond the comfortable range, nor is it mere emotional expressionism. It is like a word in an alien language that is spoken in a moment of unutterable crisis. We each feel so clearly the underlying truth and structure of meaning as we observe this gesture, yet each of our interpretations of it would be individual. This, I think, is part of the fierce and attractive beauty of this work.

And it is a prototypically theatrical truth. Who can say what the actor is thinking? More practically, as a director I cannot be entirely sure in the moment of creation what the underlying process is for the actor. Do I want to know that the actor playing Hamlet is thinking about his favorite dog who died when he was a child as he toys with Yorick's skull? Maybe in creating some postmodern romp through the material I would, but, in general the answer is "no"—I do not and perhaps cannot know what the actor is thinking when telling the story. The actor is working to create an analogy of the character's emotional reality in the experience of the audience.

Similarly, in the truly abstract nature of the gesture work, the entire body of the actor's homework and technique can be brought to the group process—made available in a usable way for the other actors. The non-linear, improvisational space that this work can generate allows many possibilities to be acted.

Gesture: Generation

Of course, it is possible to ask the actors to spend some time generating gestures on their own. But it is generally better to guide the group through a few exercises that result in gesture generation first. It is easier to modify some generated work than to stand around talking about it. After running through any of the created gestures, if the actors are in neutral it is easy to approach them with a quick comment or two designed to bring out something more of what you're looking for. What follows are not descriptions of teaching techniques. Rather, these procedures are designed to create evocative, intense, interesting acting moments with just enough structure to make them fit well into an improvisation process.

Tableaux-Technique Gesture Generation. This exercise builds gestures out of first establishing tableaux vivants or suspended stage pictures.

The first step is to ask the group to form a circle, evenly spaced, and to explain that you are going to ask them to step in, one at a time, and create a suspended pose. It is a "living sculpture" and a basic acting exercise that many of them will have done before. I ask them to think about the beginning, middle, and end of the play, choosing a particular moment and associating a word or phrase with it. If the actor is working with more than one character, then the three moments can be from more than one character. It is the basic arc of the plot, the story that needs to be told. These three moments are the subject of three tableaux.

The next step is to create the suspended sculptures in the center of the circle. One thing that needs to be stressed is the abstract nature of the pose, or suspension. A cliché will limit the actor's imagination, while an abstract gesture will free it and those of the other actors. The poses can be made into gestures, one at a time, or all three can be created first. When the improvisation is based on a particular scene, three moments in that scene can be chosen.

Then I ask the actors to create their suspension in a part of the room away from the others. I ask them to go from neutral to the pose and then right back to neutral when I say the number of the gesture/pose. Then they do it again, but this time with an exhaled breath informing the movement. The pose point is to be imagined as an elastic band or spring that bounces the actor back to neutral. Next add a sound, and the pose has become a gesture. It is short, repeatable, has a full body connection, and is fully voiced.

As the group drills the new gesture, a sense of group timing is useful and helps build the energy. It's just an improvisation form—it isn't going to perform itself. The old saying is: If you are bored, then you are boring. The imagination can be freed to inform the repetition of the gestures. One thing that helps immensely, I have found, is to remind the actor to target the gesture to another actor through the eyes. At any rate, once the gestures are informed and clear, they form the basis for the improvisation work.

Individual Generation Technique. I find that once actors have created a set of clear, useful gestures with the tableaux, and have a good feeling for them, they can simply be asked to create a set of gestures using a few minutes of rehearsal time. I just call out "time" after, say, five minutes, and ask them to drill the gestures a few times when they are finished, giving me a nod to let me know they are ready to move on. After a few drills with the whole group, it is time to move on to the full improvisation of the scene or the play.

The Nonlinear Improvisations: Gesture Improvisation Structures (Grid, Orbit) and Character Relationships

This is the dream world, or the world of images, or whatever the actor's imagination would like to call it, created in the room as a source for all of the staging and acting of the play. We cook it up out of the gestures, and it has a built-in "out" in the form of neutral, or just walking in the basic grid form. Any number of improvisations can occur in it: things that a character wishes would happen, motivations, childhood moments, all kinds of psychic, interior material externalized for the group and in the group.

As in the read-through form mentioned earlier, the group is asked to walk with an awareness of each other and each other's safety in mind, at right angles to the wall. A fast, medium, or slow pace should be a choice, it should be clear, and it should change often, as should the direction of motion. In the first step of the improvisation, the gestures are simply dropped into this frame as the actors wish, investing the rehearsal space with them. Again, this is no substitute for the actor's homework, but it can be a place to bring it all together and share it more deeply.

The second level of the nonlinear improvisation form is to not only drop the gesture into the moving room, but to focus it on another actor. Then the other actor can choose to absorb the gesture from neutral, or move through the grid, or he or she may choose to repeat the gesture back to the actor who originated it. And so the room fills with the sound and movement of these gestures being flung back and forth, amplifying the energy. This reaches a finite level. It is then time to free this energy into the cyclical, infinite nonlinear improvisation form.

And that's pretty easy to do, from the outside. Once the room is "hot" with the gestures being repeated, if the actors wish, or being dropped into the space, and the grid is keeping things moving otherwise, I just ask the actors to break the rules. When they are ready, the gestures and repetitions provoke new improvisation, bits of scene (focusing away from the actual text). They seem to know what I mean—it is not about breaking the rule to look out for each other's safety; it is about allowing improvisations to happen. Depending on what you are looking for from the tone of the play, the entire gesture work can be done without ever attaching the actual word or short phrase to the gesture, but I have more often done so. It helps provide a bridge back to the work with the text that is valuable in the staging work.

You may pause and take a break. Even when the work is productive and going well, you will often get the question, "What are we doing?" I don't think you have to actually believe in the existence of a collective subconscious to see that this work serves to build an analogy of one for the show. Many things take care of themselves, I find—things like social distance, shared social mannerisms, and especially character relationships. I will answer that question often by saying, "Concentrate on the relationships to the other character and see what happens." In a pinch, I'll just remind the actor to help fuel the others' work if they aren't finding the basic connection themselves. Placing the attention on the other actor, a basic technique of all good actors, works in nonlinear improvisation and can relax the actor into finding his or her own way.

The basic power of gorilla-theatre work is generated in these improvisations. The later stages of rehearsal channel and hone that power, but it is revisited in the paratheatrical rehearsal process, as we will see later in chapter 6.

More about Neutral

Neutral is more than just an external state. The term is a metaphor itself, inviting the actor to think about a car engine in neutral gear—the engine is still running, and it is ready to get into any other gear quickly. As I have said, it makes it possible for the director to craft exercises and improvisational forms that build upon each other instead of having to start from zero every time. It invests the rehearsal space with an atmosphere of attention and focus and concentration on the other actors that I envision as the fertile medium in which the gestural world grows.

The actors should be encouraged to keep their concentration on the other actors in their vision, either direct or peripheral, looking for what is going to come from them. In every way, the kind of openness that the great acting teachers talk about cultivating exists in the real neutral state. The actor has to be ready to move in any direction from here, to make a choice and jump right in with 100 percent, straight from neutral, with no missed beat or unfocused transition.

A few games sometimes work to help cultivate the state of neutral, and maybe even a few tricks. The games are easy to make up once you get what neutral really is. One trick that can work in the right situation is to have a tennis ball that you gently—gently!—toss to an actor between cycles of the impulse circle or in a freeze moment during an improvisation. An actor in the activated state of real neutral will catch it and toss it back to you.

Examples, Exercises, and Techniques: Work-Through

To work through the scenes, I ask that the actors have their lines memorized. Usually, this is not a problem, as they have had some improvisation on which to build some of the basic ideas and behavior of the character. From here, we can try different movement patterns, both to search for the way to tell the story in the environment and to enhance the acting to best advantage. Some movement patterns bring the improvisational discoveries into the work with the text, and this intensity is probably the best goal of the work-through process.

If the goal of the improvisation process is to bring the feel of the play into the room and to generate the multiple behavioral manifestations of the cast's imaginary world, then the goal of the work-through is to provide these with the first lines of the play's story structure. It is a vivid kind of sketching that will put us within the range of accomplishing the resolution of some complex and exact staging.

I find that the baseline of the work-through of a given scene is to just try running it straight through. I often emphasize the need for gorilla-theatre directors to allow for running scenes and interrupting the work less than usual. At the very least, if you watch, you will see more of what is going on; if you watch multiple runs of a given scene, you will notice the patterns that are appearing more consistently, and the actors will actually want to hear what you have to say when you say it.

Once the patterns begin to emerge, you will notice that some are becoming stronger and some are fading away. As the director, you need to find a way to respectfully and exactly encourage the patterns that you feel are serving the story, the gorilla-theatre show generally, and the context and the aesthetic aims of your work particularly. You must be engaged, and you must follow that engagement. The notion of "maybe people will be interested in this . . ." is not good enough, and it will never be good enough. You have to go after what works when you see it and pursue it when you feel it. The work-through is time to pay attention to the manifestations of it in the work, and to try to encourage them.

Provide tailored improvisations designed to facilitate the moments you want to transfer into the behavioral patterns that you are seeing in the simple run-throughs of the scene. Sometimes a note or two will work, but often you need to make up an imaginary scenario, sometimes even with different characters or the characters at a different age, to get the feel of what you are looking for. Once you have it, it is easy to just let the actors know that you need it to be "like that" at the moment in question. A few run-throughs will usually solidify this into a quality that the actors can work with and reproduce fairly well.

The improvisations for my production on *A Midsummer Night's Dream* have usually gone along well. The themes of the play are clear, and the needs of the characters are screamingly clear in most if not all instances. It lends itself to the nonlinear "dream" space, and the gestural world quickly takes on the life that it will need. Convincing the actors that I want that kind of intensity in the work itself sometimes takes a bit more work. It can be done, though. In the scene, late in the play, in which Hermia comes across Helena with Demetrius and Lysander, there is need, conflict, and everything intense. It usually runs a bit flat the first few times. I think this is because the male lovers most often forget that they are under a spell and need to act profoundly different from their everyday behavior. This has been clear in the improvisation; now it needs to happen in the work-through stage.

Telling them directly in notes might work, but that tends to build up to the desired amount of intensity instead of just blowing it away with too much. I'd rather go beyond my goal and then scale back as needed. So I ask them to try to play it in an improvisational way as if they were not under a spell, but as if it were a normal day, maybe at a restaurant. This makes the need to find the scene's terms pretty clear by going further in the opposite direction. I can ask the actors playing Demetrius and Lysander to pose, attempting to get Hermia's attention, and to move in front of each other—always playing the need to appear polite to Hermia

(Demetrius makes a big point about this, "though I scorn her I'll not hurt her," as he shows off for Helena), and it will all fuel Helena's reactions and her attempt to get Hermia on her side.

I can ask them to bring the qualities of animals barely restrained by fear into the improvisation, and then back into the work-through to add depth to the specific moments. As the director, your job is always to look for what the audience needs in a scene; when a moment is falling flat, you need to investigate why and work to get it supported and clear.

As you run the work-through of each scene, the actors need to understand the nature of the work. Some things will be set as you go, but nothing is final until the staging process. Here, as patterns of behavior emerge that are clear and work well, they need to be set. After a few are set, often the work in between will begin to become clear on its own, and often much that will be kept in the staging emerges here. Remember, selection is as creative a process as generation; when you see something that works in a work-through, keep it and see how it affects the rest of the scene.

Because the stage manager is on book, this can be an incredibly fertile time for character choices in the work. These choices, and the making of them, are the great work of the actors. They will need support, and I have found a very freeing and deceptively simple way to provide this. It is in the technique of asking for the line when the actor "goes up" or has forgotten the line in the rehearsal run. I simply ask them to repeat the line that they have remembered, the one just before the one they have forgotten. I ask them to make this repetition twice before they calmly call "line." Then the stage manager gives them the line. However, I find that it is very rarely necessary, if the actor is allowed to repeat the previous line. My theory is that, especially at this transitional stage of the work, the actor's subconscious is telling him or her that the line before was not given its due. The chance to "repeat" is also the chance to "re-act" the previous line in a way that is more connected to the thoughts and spirit of the character that the actor is creating right there, in real time.

It is possible to become "cool" in an emotional sense while calling "line." The process that I have described allows the entire ritual of self-recrimination to be entirely removed from the rehearsal process, and a simple system of reward and positive reinforcement replaces it. I often tell the actors that eliminating self-recrimination during rehearsal is not meant as an act of altruism, nor is it an indication that I want their anger over missed lines to be absent from the stage. Rather, I want them to understand that self-recrimination over memorization bores me entirely and moreover is something that we can agree was not the playwright's intention, nor is it ever to be a part of the work in performance. After all, the process is acting, not rote memorization or recital. And if it is not appropriate for the director to beat up on the actors, then how could it be correct for them to beat up on themselves?

As the work becomes more and more clear, as the scenes are run a number of times, it's important to make sure that you and your stage manager are moving around the perimeter of the room to observe the scenes from different vantage points. This will begin to prepare the actors for making their characters literally 360-degree creations. If you can keep an assistant or stage manager essentially 180 degrees across the space from you, this will help. If something isn't clear to you, the actor may have felt it was, and may even have been right about it, but he may have been unaware that he was pulling the energy down to one direction and eliminating the connection that much of the audience would have to the character. Brief lapses will occur and will be completely covered by the articulate, if non-verbal, reactions of the other characters. This is not the same as losing a connection to an entire block of the gorilla-theatre audience. The work-through phase is a great time to start getting the fully environmental nature of the work infused into the actors—certainly, their exposure to it will help the staging make sense more quickly.

EXAMPLES, EXERCISES, AND TECHNIQUES: STAGING

Remember that your job is to fix, not to fixate. Keep the story flowing and the actions clear. If you need to sketch in a moment and get back to it later, just let the actors know that is the case and ask the stage manager to make time for it as you finish up this phase of the work.

Often, the work will progress and a staging will unfold that works in your vision of the story. It is true that the "Why?" that an actor asks will most often have a clear and honest answer linked to the staging and the concept. But don't shy away from communicating the truth even if it is that this staging action is an arbitrary choice on your part that you just feel will work well. You will need to see these choices played out many times before you can be sure of their efficacy. Just as your first response to an actor's idea will be "Show me," the actor will usually get with the spirit of an arbitrary staging idea and work to execute it for your evaluation. The process always involves some degree of this kind of interplay.

My staging is an attempt to instill ideas of formal beauty into a highly complex and in some ways chaotic situation. The basic staging form in a park tends to be a circle. I believe that this is because in an outdoor situation audiences will tend to circle the action, much as they would gather around an interesting situation that develops in the street, or as they would form conversation groups or huddle up during a touch-football game. I believe the circling is an instinct, and I have noticed that audiences fall into recognizable patterns around the action in the park.

At a certain size, an audience will tend to create an almost perfectly formed bowl—a shape that has acoustical properties that enhance the experience. The first few rows of people will be sitting down on the ground. The next rows, standing, will leave space between themselves so that people standing farther back can gather in more tightly packed rows. It has been my observation that this form will set itself up very quickly, and in a full 360-degree shape, for an audience numbering about 500 people. This proto-shape should be kept in mind as you imagine your audience adapting to the particular topography of each of your scenes.

In bringing actors into a scene, an awareness of this adaptation will help make things go more smoothly. Do you have a stand of trees, for instance, that block immediate sight lines? It's probably a good place from which to bring characters into the scene.

My basic blocking diagram, then, consists of a circle indicating the perimeter of the scene, bisected by a line, which I bisect by another line. They meet exactly in the center and form a 90-degree angle at all four points there. I call each of these lines an axis. The rear of one axis is the "chute" from which actors enter if they are not coming directly through the audience. (The term is adopted from the circus ring.) These two lines are where the majority of strong, purposeful movement occurs. I deviate from it to indicate more emotional or less decisive states, in general. The four lines radiating out from the center point at regular angles I call simply "diagonals." In a void, these are the lines where movement of a thoughtful nature, and counter-movement based on reactions to strong, decisive action, occur. For moments or situations where organization is being imposed or an extreme reflection of hierarchy is called for, I impose a square inside the circle drawn from the points that the angles hit the perimeter and use it to guide the blocking.

Of course, no scene is completely standard or typical. However, the scene in which Macbeth and Lady Macbeth murder Duncan is probably as close to an application of this formal structure as I have made. Diagram

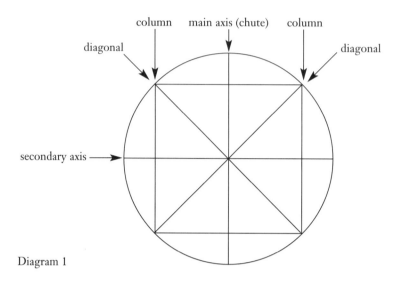

Diagram 1

1 is a shape that I adapt to most of the stage movement that I create. This diagram shows the two 90-degree crossed lines—the center line and the one that crosses it. Again, I call the first "axis" or "main axis" and the other one "secondary axis" or "cross axis." (I suppose I could call them "A" and "B" or "X" and "Y," but I don't.) The lines that cross them I call "diagonals," and the smaller lines forming a box I call "columns." The arc, a curved cross near the perimeter, is a key move because it allows a number of audience members into a close piece of an intense moment. It is also possible to move the arc closer to the center of the circle, parallel to its side. This basic pattern of movement possibilities makes the most sense to me in motion. I almost always have at least two, often more, characters moving in the action, reacting and counter-reacting with each other; keeping this pattern in mind as I do, that seems to give the work a sense of harmony.

Unlike a film director's composition, which, no matter how complex, is within a rectangular frame and made with patterns of light, your composition is truly three-dimensional, moving in time and space with a frame that is perceptual and that is induced by the behavior of the audience and the actors together. This makes for a highly complex frame, which is sensitive to mishandling but also extremely expressive and, when mastered, one that will create participatory spectacles that audiences will love. Gorilla theatre is a complicated operation for all involved, but it has a rugged ability to adapt to specific variables, and one of the reasons for this is rigorous attention to the formal beauty of the character movement.

The best way to begin to apply this careful attention is to make a detailed map of the sites that you are going to use for your production. This should be as well adjusted to scale as possible, even if you just pace out the distances. The actors and stage-management team will need copies of this diagram, described more fully in chapter 2, to help them plan transitions and layout strategies for preseting props and costume changes, if necessary. Large arrows indicating the movements of the audience and a small key showing the basic orientation of the audience for each area are helpful additions.

The next step is to make a blown-up diagram of each of the playing sites. This should be in bold, black lines with the basic topography indicated and some idea given of the orientation to the other areas. It should be on a full sheet of paper, either generated by hand or by a computer drawing program. In the corner of the page, create a box. If you have seen set or lighting plot blueprints, or storyboard cells created for film, you will recognize the box. It should have a line that states the title of the production, the name of the producing group, and the name of the park or area, and another line listing your name as director. Then, a line should say "scene" and leave a blank to fill in the scene; another line should say "text pages ___ to ___" and another for "page ___ of ___." This box needs to be on the original copy of each site diagram.

The next step is to make (or print if you are using a computer) five or ten copies of each site diagram. Three-hole punch the copies or print them onto prepunched white paper.

Next—and this is the most crucial, if also the most difficult and time-consuming step—you must go through the diagrams and, at each site, draw out your blocking patterns with close reference to the script. At the very least, you must have the scouting photographs of the sites with you to visualize the motion. Of great help here will be your impressions and notes on the improvisation and work-through that you have done with the actors. As your site diagram gets crowded with arrows and other indications of the movement, switch to a fresh copy, marking the first one "1 of __" and so on until you have a complete narrative of the scene's motion that you can convey to the actors clearly. When you finish, go back and fill in the blank "of ___" as you will be able to count back how many pages it took you to describe the motions and action. For instance, your five pages of blocking on act one, scene three, will each have a tag in the box indicating that they are "page 1 of 5," "page 2 of 5," "page 3 of 5," and so on, making it easy to see the sequence of the action diagrams.

As you are creating the diagrams, it is imperative that you visualize the action in the site, including all exits, entrances, and cues. Exits and entrances, often added by well-meaning editors along with other staging notes, must be corrected to work along the lines of your gorilla-theatre staging. For instance, the editors of most Shakespeare texts place a "Demetrius exits" note *after* Helena's line "in the temple, in the field you do me mischief . . ." line. In my work-through and paratheatric rehearsal one year, Demetrius was already running off, and this line was called after him by a despondent Helena; the rest of the line flowed as an observation to herself, leading beautifully into the following monologue. I indicated this in the blocking diagram, and everything went smoothly into performance.

Developing the diagrams will increase your knowledge of the action and add to the detail of your visualization. As you take the actors through the action, I suggest that you go back and let them walk through it at comfortable intervals. Every once in a while, they will find a discrepancy, and you will need to fix it so that the action flows smoothly. This happens to architects, too, and sometimes the most complex building plan ends up with a wall diagrammed a few inches off. The staging rehearsal is not a test of your knowledge of the action; it is a time for you to deploy it and get everyone moving along toward run-throughs.

You must be familiar enough with the patterns and staging to move along in describing it ahead of the actors' ability to get it all down. Ask them to stop you when they need to catch up, and give them time to run the pieces that they have gotten down. Assurance on your part is imperative. Learning this assurance hinges on your familiarity with the vision you have mapped out. Also, I have found it useful to observe the actions of master painters, Jackson Pollock in particular (there are short films available of him working on a painting), and of sail-makers—specifically, the phase of the process when the sail-maker pins the shape of the new sail to the workshop floor with a series of knives that he throws down as he moves over the new sail's shape. You will see how an artist makes shapes in material, and you can carry this confidence into your work, which is essentially shaping behavior in time.

Here are two examples of staging diagrams. As I say, an exact circle is rare. However, in the first two years of *Macbeth* at Fort Tryon Park in New York City, the first scene between Macbeth and Lady Macbeth was about as close to a circle as you could come. A basic move is indicated by

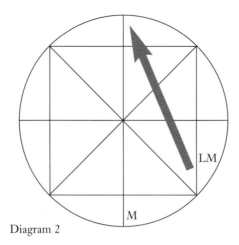

Diagram 2

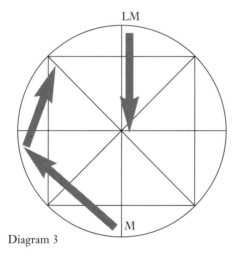

Diagram 3

an arrow (diagram 2). A second move is shown with a hypothetical coun-termove (diagram 3). The moves take on a particular idea of beauty that is specifically mine; yours will reflect your sensibilities quite transpar-ently without a forced effort to do so. The styles that I call arc, angle, line, axis, and column become a kinetic visual vocabulary that the audi-ence feels and reads along with the acting and the larger framing ele-ments. Early in the play, the vocabulary is laid out as a part of the char-acter exposition and plot genesis. It doesn't look artificial—it is a stylization crafted to help tell the story. And the variations on these individual style vocabularies then become a kind of behavioral spotlight, bringing special attention to the moment when necessary and when used properly. One director who had heard a thing or two about my work from an actor I had cast once decided to make the grid his staging system for a whole play. It was a uniform decision imposed on the whole show and it was so quickly understood by both the actors and the audience that it was almost as quickly disliked.

You will see that each scene that you are staging has its own demands. There is a musiclike build and structure that you will need to pay close attention to. The dynamics of behavior, the phrasing of movement and story, and all of the elements that make gorilla theatre are brought together most fundamentally in the staging. Furthermore, the fact of the audience's motion is at once so simple and at the same time so completely endemic to the work that it provides a unique torsion and unique opportunities as well. The staging is in harmonious counterpoint to the other behavioral "voices" at work—those of the playwright, the actors, and the audience.

Run-Throughs

I have often had actors note that our rehearsal process has brought them to the point where they feel ready to open a show well ahead of opening night. This is the right place to have a show, before the paratheatric rehearsal (explained later in full) brings its new dimensions to the production. Run through, run through, and run through again—it adds the polish you need. Nothing puts a gorilla-theatre production right where it needs to be quite like opening night, of course, but run-throughs are even more important for an aesthetic designed to work with the audience.

It is hard for me to think of these run-throughs as rehearsal, really. They are performed for an imaginary audience—a very taxing process for the actors. It puts burdens on them that are different from the rest of the rehearsal preparation.

From my experience, there is no question that the last rehearsal before opening is the most difficult of all for a well-rehearsed gorilla-theatre production. Even if it seems to go flawlessly, this in itself points up in even greater relief the biggest flaw possible—the audience is missing! The show is built like a table missing two legs, waiting precariously for them to be nailed on.

The audience provides that essential element—all the rehearsal and technique in the world still does not create anything like theatre unless there's an audience there. The underlying structure of the staging movement and the governing principles of each aesthetic decision and execution demand the reception and understanding of the audience, and so it becomes odd that they are not there—since so much energy is being poured into the work.

Even the simple fact of the motion of the audience from place to place, which is so individual to each audience's experience of the gorilla-theatre production, communicates truth to that audience. And everything that is so deeply discovered and painstakingly brought to light by the actors needs a place to rest in the audience's experience, received by them simultaneously on so many levels, and this is then processed by the actors into the fabric of the show. It is a gorilla-theatre phenomenon that results in many wonderful things.

A general principle to remember is this: run through the show indoors, but do a mark-through of the show outdoors. On your site, it will be made more difficult, but with no real reward, to perform without an audience to experience the gorilla theatre. Running from entrance to exit and scene-site change to scene-site change is useful, of course, with the dialogue marked or sped through—passersby will ask for information on the show. It is better to save the real thing for going through with a real audience on opening night. That just makes it even clearer that the total experience is a newly minted thing and that the maximum energy and concentration must be put into it for it to work right and make that gorilla-theatre magic.

Adapting Indoor Techniques to Outdoor Uses

As noted at the beginning of the chapter, you should use what you know. Keeping the ultimate goal of the gorilla production in mind will change your demands on the indoor exercises and techniques that you use here, of course. Helping the actors make a supersaturated performance, to keep in touch with the real and fluid nature of the frame in gorilla theatre, is important and will change the work you do with them. Still, a few basic considerations are worth noting.

The difference between speaking with power and yelling cannot be overstated. Still, as you get more and more power in your rehearsal room, you will sometimes find that your work is more interesting to the people working in the studio next door than their own work is. This will make them jealous and, rather than redoubling their efforts to be interesting and to concentrate, they will interrupt you instead. Sometimes you just have to ask the actors to scale back the sheer volume, while maintaining the intense focus. A basic gesture drill that Kevin Kuhlke used was to create the gesture at a lesser overall percentage—both of volume and range of motion—while maintaining the gesture's integrity.

There are many ways to help actors build their character in rehearsal, and I will assume that you are familiar with a broad range of them. Often all that is necessary to adapt them to gorilla theatre is to do these familiar exercises before and after the gesture work, which provides actors with a sense of the scale. Don't indulge in the sloppy thinking of calling gorilla theatre "big" or "broad" theatre—those who do will lose the precious delicacy of connection to the audience that real detail brings. So, then, even a delicate and internal exercise like the internal monologue can bring the actors' homework together in a useful way. I'll use it as an example.

The classic internal monologue improvisation is similar to a verbal form of automatic writing. For those of you who didn't have to do it in English class, automatic writing consists of putting pen to paper and not stopping until a certain prearranged time has passed. The idea is to write and write, never stopping or pausing to reflect, even if it means you need to repeat a word or phrase over and over. It is a window into the creative process that translates well into the rehearsal process. Even the technique itself can be used to enhance the rehearsal process to great effect—I often ask actors to attempt automatic writing for three- to five-minute sessions after a particularly deep gesture improvisation. It has provided the actors with unexpectedly useful notes for use later in the process.

The internal monologue exercise consists of the actors walking in the grid, as at the beginning of the gesture work. In the first phase, the actors talk automatically; that is, they are told never to pause but to keep talking and see what comes out, even if it means repeating a word or phrase. It is an imaginary monologue using the character's desires and experiences as a starting point. I ask the actors to talk about what the character wants, where they are coming from, and where they are going. In this first phase, there is no dialogue—the actors may use the sight of each other to visualize the other characters, but it is a monologue of the characters speaking to themselves.

When the internal monologue exercise is working, the room becomes a buzz of intensity. You will learn over time how to sense when this exercise is being used effectively. Pay close attention to the actors, and you will see a new light on the character work coming to life. When this has been effective, a second phase can involve bits of dialogue—broken and incomplete—and evocative exchanges can occur. Sometimes, later in the process, I use the internal monologue as a warm-up to the gestural work, and it seems to help bring the detailed, internal connections of the actors together with the power and energy necessary for gorilla theatre.

A Note

Sometimes I have found that, at certain points in rehearsal, nothing seems to be happening for an actor—at least not from their point of view. But it is. In a way, they are working so hard that it seems easy. It is like sailing, when you turn into the wind and let the sail way out. It's called "running," and you're going the same direction as the wind. Have you done that? After all of the wind and spray you feel when working against the wind, you turn and put the wind to your back, and then suddenly everything seems so still. There doesn't seem to be any wind at all, and you seem to be standing still, but it's just because you are going in the same direction and the same speed as the wind. The trees on shore are moving quickly, if you look there. To an actor who is doing well, but feels like she isn't "doing" anything, I ask: Are you at one of those moments? You are as full of this play as a sweeping white sail is full of the moving air. As the director of a gorilla-theatre show, it is important to know that an actor who is new to the aesthetic will have a lot to digest at first. When actors are working well, the learning will be done and they will know a lot about what works, and it will become more unself-conscious to them.

chapter **six**

The Paratheatric Rehearsal Technique

Brief Description

Jerzy Grotowski's famous "paratheatric" experiments in the '60s and '70s were a breakthrough in their time, a watershed in the history of the relationship between audience and spectacle. Scholarship and reportage abound on his attempts to fuse audience and cast in ritual events, and I will not attempt to duplicate it here. Let me say here that I in no way criticize Grotowski's paratheatrics. In fact, naming my technique the "paratheatric *rehearsal*" is meant as both a direct homage to his work and a means of making a distinction from it.

In a paratheatric rehearsal, the cast takes some time to live together and concentrate directly on the play at hand, using the relative freedom and isolation of a rural setting. I have always found that trees, meadows, hillsides, and beaches allow the imagination full freedom to grow and add to the rehearsal process. Any farm or beach or tract of wild land can serve as a location for your paratheatric rehearsal.

One of the reasons that the paratheatric rehearsal is of vital importance to outdoor avant-garde gorilla theatre is that the environment provokes work on the proper scale. I mean scale of imagination, fully formed physicality, and vocal power. Now, I have heard a whisper at fifty yards when executed properly, so I'm not talking about yelling. I'm talking about directed communication and storytelling in the environmental mode.

In the paratheatric rehearsal process, the cast gets the chance to be its own first audience in the fully realized environmental improvisation. Dashing from scene-site to scene-site, transforming into and out of character with full intensity, the cast returns to the improvisational flow that began the whole process. They also get an object lesson from the rest of the cast in the intensity needed to pull off this style of work—and an example of it to take with them back to the audiences who will enjoy their gorilla work.

The paratheatric exercises give a new channel to the imagination's flow and to the shared experience of the work. The fabled "bonding experience" so often taken as a commonplace of cast life and in most productions amounting to little more than a noisy night of drinking is transformed into a work of great merit by paratheatric rehearsal.

My early experiments with paratheatric rehearsal may give you a guide to start a few of your own experiments before you depart on a full paratheatric rehearsal retreat. The fully articulated system that I talk about in the rest of this chapter is the outgrowth of these early experiments, and they have been tested on numerous shows to date. They've always been a lot of hard work, but the results are undeniable. You can use the technique to great advantage.

There will always be the safety net of established blocking and rehearsal to fall back on, and the tools of story and character that have been formed, but using these paratheatric techniques, set patterns get blown out, tested, and looked at from a new perspective. The production is brought to life in a safe test area and the process yields incendiary new material to fuel the production run.

Early Experiments

I first became fascinated with the notion that shared experience is what is seen onstage between actors after seeing the results of some intense rehearsal and scene work that Kevin Kuhlke was doing at the Experimental Theatre Wing. Much has been written about memory and imagination in acting techniques. I decided that I needed to focus on a way for the actors to bring together, in a dynamic way, the results of their work apart, in a shared process for the production as a whole; the gesture work is the result of that, and so is the paratheatric rehearsal.

The first paratheatric notion I can remember having (other than wondering if the exercises that Andre Gregory describes in *My Dinner with Andre* could be put to practical use in a rehearsal process) was a joke I made up while rehearsing *Hamlet*, my senior thesis at New York

University. I was a bit frustrated with the banal way that everyone's characters were acting around supposed corpses. Ophelia's body, even Yorick's skull were just not being treated as heightened in the way that I knew that they would need to be to give the compelling performance that I was looking for.

So, I jokingly told the cast members that we would be having a special rehearsal at the city morgue, to give them exposure to corpses so that they would have a memory to work with on stage. The joke turned into a rumor, and the rumor begat a buzz that could not be stopped about odd goings-on in the *Hamlet* rehearsal room. The gesture work was going full force, so tales of the intensity of these rehearsals were already spreading.

Instead of going to the morgue, we honed the work on the specific scenes. In the case of Ophelia's corpse, I asked the actors to circle around the actress, who lay still under a cloth. I had given each actor a flower, and as they circled I asked them to engage in really reacting to the idea of death—her death in the story, but also whatever process they needed to go through with memory or other techniques. I asked them to drop their flower on the covered "corpse" as soon as they had established an honest emotional connection to this work. As the last flower dropped, I signaled Hamlet and Horatio, who had been observing from behind some rehearsal cubes, that the scene would begin.

The scene ran with the necessary intensity. At a certain point, as Hamlet and Laertes were going back and forth, I noticed that Horatio was particularly agitated—he was really trying to interpose himself between the funeral party and Hamlet's wild talk. I also watched Gertrude, who had a strong bond to Ophelia's corpse that seemed to me to be maternal and very deep. As Hamlet lept into the "grave" I realized what had freaked out poor Horatio—as Hamlet had been hurling his darts at Laertes, he had been tearing off his clothes and was now jumping on Ophelia's poor shrouded corpse completely naked!

The scene finished up, the actor got dressed, and we all discussed the results. It was all right with everyone to keep this in the show, and so we did, to great effect.

I wanted to give the actors a new connection to this kind of early improvisational freedom later in the process, and the paratheatrical rehearsal was designed as a crucible for this.

Scouting and Booking

Getting an advance team to the paratheatric rehearsal location has proven to be an effective way to ensure a smooth process. My first paratheatric rehearsal, for my production of *Hamlet*, in 1990, started off with the entire cast arriving in a van, with a couple of sacks of groceries. There were logistical complications, but, fortunately for us, we had a friend along who was not in the cast who agreed to cook.

I had found the space for the paratheatric rehearsal looking in the classified ads. The May dates for our work were after the ski season had ended, and we found a small farmhouse in upstate New York that the producer felt we could afford. How I convinced him and the owner of the farm that this was all a rational idea, I don't recall exactly. But after seeing some pictures of the space and ascertaining that there was enough open land and available woods, the deal was sealed and paid for in cash. I picked up the key, and we all piled into a rented sixteen passenger van to make what was supposed to be a three-hour trip to our location. A few wrong turns and a flat tire later, an exhausted crew pulled up to the farm to rest up a bit before getting to work.

If you have the chance, scout your location beforehand. In this instance, and in others over the years, pictures of the land and a good idea that it can accommodate the work have proven to be true guides. My second paratheatric rehearsal was on a farm that my family owned in Cumberland, Virginia—somewhat farther away than the first location but more affordable, as I didn't have a producer on hand. My parents generously provided food for the cast and crew that summer, and the following summer as well. Both times we were performing *A Midsummer Night's Dream*, and in both instances we added a public performance to the schedule, the evening following the paratheatric-rehearsal run. The first year's show was performed on and around the farm itself, and a few of my relatives attended. The second year's performance was more widely enjoyed by people in the county, as it was held in, on, and around the courthouse lawn in the center of town. In the years since, many other wonderful locations for paratheatrics have been donated and have helped the work tremendously.

Logistics

Paratheatric rehearsals are a lot of work. I want to acknowledge how much fun they are, and at the same time make it clear that this very fact can be deceptive. Everyone needs to understand their responsibilities well and be ready to make things happen with a great outpouring of energy. I have been approached to direct shows for other companies, ones outwardly similar to mine. My first question: Do I get to cast the show? Often, there is some hemming and hawing—don't I like the actors in their company? Invariably I do, or I wouldn't be asking the question. Do you see my point? The very most fundamental values affect the outcome. The same is true with paratheatric rehearsals. I have been asked to conduct those, too, although I am skeptical of directors who don't want to run the rehearsals themselves.

I ask the following question of groups who want me to run paratheatrics for them: Are you ready to ban drugs and alcohol from the paratheatric rehearsal? So far, that has been a successful test of their ability to commit to the work. They say no, and spread rumors about my work ethic, if I'm lucky, or about what a tight-ass I am if I'm not so lucky. But I always hear back from those casts that while the rehearsal was a great party, it had little or nothing to do with the rehearsal process and yielded no clear results. After the paratheatric rehearsal is over, usually the last thing I do before leaving the space, is declare the work complete, congratulate the cast, and proceeded to host a congratulatory celebration at which there is, as in the case of the first *Midsummer* work, a lot of cold beer to be had. The value is on finishing the work properly; if we had not, we would have used the time allocated for the party to finish the work. Rule number one about logistics: Get your priorities straight, and your task list and time-allotment strategies will follow. Sometimes the best celebration is a good night's sleep.

Schedule

The model paratheatric-rehearsal weekend retreat adheres to the following schedule:

Friday, in the evening, the cast arrives at the site. Whatever time is left when they arrive, which is usually after dinner, is spent getting sleeping arrangements worked out. The best way that I can think of to ruin a good paratheatric rehearsal would be to have a party and get drunk on

Friday night. I request that all paratheatrics be free of alcohol and drugs. Perhaps it is not a coincidence that all of my paratheatrics to date have been successful ones.

On Saturday, preparatory exercises are proposed and created. Saturday morning after breakfast and before lunch is a good time for extensive warm-up and exercises designed to enhance scale and presence in the outdoor environment. The time after lunch is spent on more production-specific improvisations. After dinner, there is usually a break, unless the cast could benefit from a straight line-through. Later, a bonfire is lit, and specific exercises tailored to this environment are conducted, targeted at deepening the storytelling abilities of the cast in relation to the story at hand.

On Sunday morning, breakfast is a bit later—more of a brunch really—then, after a thirty-minute period for digestion and vocal warm-up, the cast warms up fully together and performs the paratheatric run. Because it is important to get the paratheatric run off in one piece if at all possible, the later meal helps free up the block of time. The original paratheatric run for *Hamlet* took eight hours! The later breakfast/brunch helps prepare the cast for the long outburst of energy that this technique requires. During a *Twelfth Night* paratheatric, the cook who was helping us left snacks for us in the kitchen—delicious cookies, as I recall—and not only did actors run there and back for refueling but, at one point, Sir Toby and Sir Aguecheek took the action there. This allowed me to grab a cookie on the run, as Sir Aguecheek used a plate of powdered sugar to indicate lines of cocaine as he said the line "I have it in my nose, too." Great moment—not that it made it into the performance—but I was grateful for the laugh and the snack. Later on Sunday, I highly recommend a warm-down period. I ask the actors not to discuss the work for seventy-two hours after it is completed. The urge to talk about every discovery is channeled, in the warm-down period, into writing in their notebooks. I ask that a period of silence be respected for this time. Some fall immediately to sleep—the work is exhausting. Others write feverishly and, it seems to me, to great effect. Others do some combination of the two. And because the work is so often performed in beautiful, sylvan surroundings, some add a quiet, reflective walk around the grounds to their warm-down period. After that, it is onto the bus, or off to the train station, or whatever the travel arrangements are. Sunday dinner is usually cold sandwiches carried along or fast food on the road.

There is no official schedule for Monday, but in the ideal schedule the cast gets the Monday after the paratheatric retreat off. It takes some time for the subconscious to absorb what has often been an exhausting experience. Also, we all need positive reinforcement, especially American artists who live in a country so hostile and often oblivious to the need for their work. A hot bath and a good rest on the Monday after a paratheatric rehearsal is, to my mind, a very good addition to the schedule. As I often say, any day that an actor takes to sleep in, eat well, take a hot bath, and, at most, work on their lines, is a day that is an important contribution to the show.

The paratheatric run makes the procedure special, that is the key point. All points may be changed and adapted to circumstance and the creative nature of the process except this one: without the paratheatric run of the show you have had perhaps a retreat, perhaps even a productive one, but not a truly paratheatric rehearsal.

Blazing and Establishing Safe Practices

Bug spray! It helps to take some basic precautions. Seriously, working outdoors is not the lark that it seems at first. As anyone experienced in outdoor sports will tell you, preparation is important. If you are working in the Northeast, long pants, shoes and socks, and bug repellent are very important. During the development of the paratheatric rehearsal process, Lyme disease began to spread in the areas where I was working at the time. It was a good thing I had been briefed on the symptoms—I ended up contracting it. Fortunately, I got to a doctor in time and recovered. Still, it was no fun giving the notes from that paratheatric run while lying on my back in pain. Additionally, you should have a first-aid kit on hand and know the phone numbers for the local fire department, ambulance, and police. There will always be some bumps and bruises—it's a good idea to bring along extra aspirin, cold packs, and ace bandages. Water should be available all the time, especially during the paratheatric run and especially if you are working in the heat. Sunscreen is also very important, and I hope you have some shade to work in.

To demonstrate which areas are safe to work in, and approved for your work by the hosts of your paratheatric rehearsal, I suggest an exercise called blazing. Compared by some to a walking meditation, blazing is simple, but it can and should take more time than you might think. As

I will explain later, the paratheatric run will have the freedom to move to various sites. Blazing establishes which sites are available for use. To blaze, the director moves around the location, pausing at each stage area. The actors keep the director in sight and quietly explore the space when the director pauses. The exercise is completed in silence, unless an emergency arises. With a group paying the right kind of attention, this exercise can really load the imagination with possibilities for the work.

Anyone who attempted a task beyond their physical ability would be considered foolish. Such needless risks are unnecessary in paratheatric rehearsal work as well. Everyone must be relied on to work within their range. That the safety of the cast and crew are the top priority needs to be said, said again, and practiced. Sometimes things will happen in the routine and prosaic course of things that will require this value to be strongly repeated.

For example, here's a story I call "Lady M Goes for a Run." Our Lady Macbeth that year was a marathon runner in great shape, especially considering that she was a relatively new mother. In addition to being talented, she was a bit headstrong (not uncommon in the arts, of course) and, in my opinion, a little scared of this unknown procedure. She had plenty of information about the work, and I had written a long letter to the cast about the process, a tried-and-true one at that point. She seemed fine with it on the way to the site.

When we got there, I could tell that she had made a deal with herself, and that she was going to approach the work on her own terms. I thought, so be it, as long as the work gets done. In this case, it was her running schedule that she was adamant about preserving. Now, when I say "adamant," it sounds as if I were giving her some resistance to her idea of running a few miles early in the morning. I was not. If only the whole cast should be so disciplined! When she saw that I was more than happy to hear that she would be out running, she said she would be back in time for the beginning of the paratheatric run and not to hold breakfast for her or worry about her at all.

When she was thirty minutes late for her call, I knew something was wrong and I did, in fact, begin to worry. But this was not passive worrying; this was Gorilla Rep worrying. Which meant that the cast was quickly divided into three squads, one for each car that we had plus the van, which I rode in. Also, as luck would have it, we had three cast members who were from the area. One of these was included in each squad. We made sure that each squad had a cell phone, and we left one member back at the house to call if she should turn up, and to call the local police to let them know we were worried. This was an independent, strong-willed woman, and I was sure she would be doing whatever she could to get back early, not just on time, so I really was worried.

The squads departed for their cars and we took off, having agreed on a search pattern that would cover about as far as we thought she could have gotten and working back in from the perimeter. As my team rolled, I called the local hospitals to leave her description in case she should be admitted to the emergency room unconscious.

Well, "Lady M Goes for a Run" has a happy ending. About half an hour or so into the search, base camp back at the house called to say that Lady M had returned, having gotten good and lost, having had a good cry by the roadside, and getting a ride back to the house from a local family on their way to soccer practice. She had retained the calm required to recall the address of the house and had been duly delivered.

This was a cast that understood that safety meant looking out for each other. The rest of the paratheatric rehearsal went famously, and the production went on to run for five years after getting a great notice in the *New York Times*.

Improvisation Suggestions for Day One and Day Two

On Day One, there is so much to do to develop the scale and depth of exploring in the new mode. The basic gesture work takes on a whole new tone outdoors. I start with the impulse circle, slowly expanding the circle until it is fifty yards across. In a handy field, usually, I like to take the cast through the entire gestural-world building process. It usually goes more quickly, but it also seems infused with new possibilities. As I see these possibilities arise, like faces in the clouds, I work to give the group forms that will encourage the exploration of these possibilities. An early improvisation was a pantomime war between the Amazons and their queen and Theseus and his warriors for *A Midsummer Night's Dream*. The real juice began to flow when we added supernatural warrior powers to the game and created alternative endings. After improvising that Hippolyta wins and takes Theseus prisoner, and many other alternatives, the actress playing the Amazon queen had a new fire in her eyes as the captive of the court scene that opens the play. She had given herself as a sacrifice to save her people, as it turned out in the improvisation, and was no mere war trophy. This set up a whole new arc for the love between

Hippolyta and Theseus to grow out of admiration for good judgment and a shared knowledge of political power and its intricacies. The fairies in that play improvised physical work in and around the trees. And the Claudius family in *Hamlet* had an improvised picnic at one point in that paratheatric rehearsal. Day One leads in to the night's bonfire work, which I will describe in the next section.

On Day Two, the warm-up and crescendo to the paratheatric run is the key, the cornerstone, the apex. This is a time for adding some structural bones to the flesh and blood developed the day and night before. The sculpture of the morning is to be shaped more closely to improvising the actual events of the play, but in a nonlinear way. A circular truth, moving back over covered ground to spiral into the nightmares, dreams, fears, hopes, and desires that fuel the action of the play. If the performance is the metaphorical canvas to be painted every night, and the first day and night are the primitive grinding of the new pigment powders to make the paint, then the second day is the time to invoke the gallons and gallons of paint that will be poured and washed and brushed over the canvas to make the vivid, rich gorilla-theatre style what it is.

The Bonfire: Metaphor and Practice

You build a fire. It is a gradual process, when done correctly. You start with one match and lay it to some tinder. Before this, you have dug away the turf and set it aside to cover the spot later. The small hollow also protects the tinder from the wind so that it can catch more easily. Buckets of water and a fire extinguisher are nearby in case any accident should occur. Everyone else is on break, so it is a moment to be alone and become centered and composed. The patience that the rehearsal process needs it not unlike the patience necessary to build a fire. It will be a size that you might think of as more of a campfire, but as a metaphor for the actors it will blaze as countless fires have blazed since the beginning of the species, to burn and lend the imagination a bright and swirling fuel.

Earlier, either by yourself or with a few others, you have gathered up firewood, broken it into manageable pieces, and stacked these pieces by size. Much later, when the work is done, and perhaps the cast is taking a brief break before bed to toast marshmallows and hang around the fire or even, sometimes, to increase the energy level before the nights work, I pile dry pine on the fire crosswise, resulting in hot flames that leap far up and over the pile of scraps. Then, I get a good running start and leap over them. I usually get a few hairs singed off of my legs, but it is fun and one of the only chances I get to participate in the doing of things. It is showing off, to be sure, but also entertaining for the cast. I like to think it sets people at ease who are less used to campfires like this, but this may be a personal illusion.

As you build your fire, setting each larger set of sticks onto it carefully—never, ever throwing them on but always placing them on—this metaphor for your role in the process should be clear. As you place the sticks, the fire burns better. As you explain the exercises to the cast, they burn better. Sometimes a damp stick takes time to catch. Sometimes a reluctant actor needs time to work in the exercise, to get inside it, to burn. Gesturing through the flames . . . the symbol Antonin Artaud used for the truth of acting in his important work *The Theater and Its Double*, but to me the actors become flames themselves. The performance is fed dry fuel by the participation of the audience, by their attention and care. This gives the actors the energy to throw their light and heat back at the audience, and the cycle grows through the progress of the performance. I think back to the moments of building fires on beaches, in parks, and in fields, the summoning of the actors to swim in the nuances of the setting sun and the rising flames, creating new work at the end of what would have been a traditional rehearsal process. For all of its delicacy and detail, the theatre is the first art form, storytelling inspiring singing, and painting, and so on. There is a directness and a power of communication in the theatre that no other form can imitate. Here, around the fire that you build, the actors can find pathways to the pancultural roots of the form, and can articulate them into the most current expression of it. Here we master the fire, we tell stories as in every theatre, and in every gorilla-theatre production. You invite the actors to join you by the fire, and they bring the fire to the audience in their work.

Night Exercises

FEAR OF THE DARK

The "Fear of the Dark" exercise was originally designed for *A Midsummer Night's Dream*'s paratheatric rehearsal. The theory was that fairies come from our fear of the dark and our personalization of that fear. I asked the actors to use the exercise to find that fear and recognize it, work with it, and see what it had to say about fairies. The Fear of the

Dark exercise is performed around bonfire with a good area of woods surrounding it. Here is its basic form, and I'll discuss modifications after this description.

The group is called to stand in a circle around the fire. The basic instructions are explained. It is, as always, up to the actors to work within parameters that are safe for them, and only they can know what those are. These are the instructions:

1. When I ask you to begin, turn your back to the fire and begin walking away from it. Walk slowly and stay in control.
2. At all times, move gently away from another actor if you come near them, especially at the very beginning of the exercise.
3. The horn will be blown in exactly five-minute increments; you are asked never to go beyond the sound of the horn.
4. As you move into the woods, be aware of your feelings. When you feel fear strongly, stop.
5. Find out what the fear is like, move, breathe, but maintain silence vocally.
6. If you are in trouble and need help at any time, break the silence and call "cut!" loudly. The exercise then ends and we will find and help you. Likewise, if you hear someone call "cut!" drop the exercise and move toward him or her to help.
7. As you move with the fear and explore it, see if you can guide it to the purpose of the work, or the character, or the story, however you think of it.
8. Later, as we move past the halfway point in the exercise, you may run into another actor in the improv space that has been created. See what happens. Either one of you can always move away.
9. The horn will be blown in three short bursts at the middle of the exercise period (after fifteen minutes).
10. The horn will be blown continuously at the end of the exercise in bursts. When you hear this, return to the fire, remaining silent and inside the work. We will remain silent until everyone has returned, a few minutes more, then "end" will be declared.

As always, it is good practice to refrain from discussing the exercise immediately afterward. Time should be afforded for the actors to record their impressions in their notebooks.

The Fear of the Dark exercise itself changes at the direction of the actor. Upon learning of the fear in the woods, the actor can guide the improvisational aspect of the work. However, it can be guided from without as well. Calling it "Fairy Construction" and noting the subconscious-origin theory of fairies guides the exercise for, say, *A Midsummer Night's Dream*.

Also, variations with candles can be tried. This is a more introspective version and worked well for a *King Lear* cast. The cast members carried candles with them and moved all about nighttime meadow quite freely. As they finished carefully but briefly looking into the eyes of each other character, they then ventured out into the dark woods. As soon as they felt the fear, they blew out their candles. Lear was the last one left to walk into the woods, alone. In the dark field, Lear looked around for company, lost in his thoughts and loneliness. It was poignant and fed the actor's work with the isolation of Lear in the latter part of the play. When he blew out his candle, the action's association with death was inescapable.

TELL THE TALE

Standing around the fire at a comfortable distance, the cast tells the story of the play by each saying a word, one at a time. My brother and I used to make up stories this way. It is important to stay focused, but it can be really fun once it gets up to speed. It should finish up pretty quickly. Now, right when the cast thinks they have been clever about telling the story, ask them to do it again but this time as their characters, completely trying to spin the story with their character's bias. At many points, the crucial word about an event will get to a character who has a lot invested in how the story is told, and under these circumstances the efforts to get the story done are fascinating.

A variation on this is to have each character tell the story of the play either from the point of view of being dead and looking back on the events, or from before the play occurs, narrating the desires they have as they go into it. It is important to remember not to allow the actors to mediate the truth. This is best achieved by appealing to their sense of drama. If two characters agree that one is right, the drama is flattened. This kind of exercise is a chance to alternate as audience for each other in a new way.

Rhythm and Dance

Bringing a few drums and small percussion instruments along on a paratheatric is often a good idea—especially if you are working in an isolated area. Around the bonfire, everything from the obvious dance and chant of the witches in *Macbeth* to all kinds of fairy-building work can be enhanced with members who are sitting out of the work to play the percussion. It helps to have a few experienced drummers in the lot, but as long as the beat is kept simple, anyone can usually pick it up just fine. The basic feel of the simple beat often allows more room for the imagination to play as well. Titania falling asleep after a dance with Bottom and the fairies in *A Midsummer Night's Dream* has proven interesting in this form. Once the fairies are built and can move around, the question of how they dance is important as well.

As in all of the work, the feelings that the night work evokes are important, as is the directorial sculpting of the event to hone its usefulness to the gorilla-theatre production. It is fun, that is clear, but it is revelatory theatre work as opposed to simple revelry.

The Paratheatric Run

The paratheatric run is the heart of the paratheatric rehearsal process. Simply put, it consists of the actors in each scene deciding, with as few words as possible, where they will play the scene. Then, to complete the form, they run the scenes in these places, in order, exploring each site while using the scene as a tool to do so. Earlier, the blazing process has established the safe physical parameters for the work. Within these, and often with amazing results, the scenes are played. These results inform the gorilla show, as we will see, in at least three ways: first, in the blocking changes that can be brought back, second in new acting discoveries, and third in the fantastic once-only experiences that can't be duplicated for later audiences but that give the assembled artists a shared history.

Previously set stage movement is disregarded, and in each scene the cast explores the qualities of the sire that the actors have chosen. In every scene, in every moment, the question is addressed: What appears to be new here? In an environment dedicated to exploration, new reactions and new risks can make a kind of alchemy that exists nowhere else.

The paratheatric run uses the text of the play exclusively and strives to tell its story here, in the new setting and situation. There may be rewriting experiments, adaptation, or translation workshops to be done, perhaps in a modified form of the paratheatric run. For the purposes of this work, the true text needs to be used to provide the through-line and cohesion that the depth of experimentation on other levels needs. When I say "true text" I simply mean the text that will be used in the gorilla-theatre production with an audience.

There is an attitude of attention and fun, playfulness with serious-minded intent, that pervades the paratheatric rehearsal run. It is impossible to make an artistic mistake here. Sure, risks are run, and it is imperative to keep everyone safe. Take care of yourself and watch out for the others. Most of all, your example as the director is important. I ran so hard to get to each scene in my first paratheatric run! It was amazing to see the new form unfold, and to watch the actors catch fire with all of the creative possibilities that were taking over the process. As I continue to go as fast as I can from scene to scene, my flat-out speed may have diminished, but my enthusiasm hasn't. Acting is a wonderful, exciting thing to see to begin with, but watching it run untrammeled through the countryside, painting the hills with imagination, is thrilling.

The director is the one person who experiences the entire story from the outside, even though it surrounds him as he is running through it. (This is the only time that "run-through" is literal!) Guard your experiences with your disciplined attention—if ever there was a time for economical, clear notes, this would be it. A video camera can capture an image, but it can't judge the impact of the emotional and physical choices that are made.

We have brought a videographer along on a few of the paratheatric runs. For me, the videotape has served as a record after the work was done, but it never supplants notes to the actors. My notes have provided a practical bridge back to the gorilla-theatre work itself after the explosion of the paratheatric run. When present, a videographer is helped by the director to get from scene to scene as the paratheatric run progresses. We never stop the run for battery changes but made them on the fly. Later in the week, after the three-day period is over, the cast enjoys seeing the video record of the work and it does no harm at all. They have, after all, worked very hard, and a reminder of the work is useful just before opening. In the case of *Sailing to Byzantium*, the videotape of the initial paratheatric experiments that started the rehearsal process became a part of the show.

Here are a few notes for an actor during the paratheatric run: As you work, ask yourself questions, as an actor, and your work itself will ask questions of the other actors. Questions like: "What changes here? The smell of boxwood—does it set off something in you? The dry air in the barn—can you feed that to the character? You let the feelings move through you—remember, the character and blocking are there. We can always recall and go back to them. They are like a safety net. There is a slope here, and a tree that can hide me—what can my character use here to accomplish my goals? How does it feel to use it? You let the feelings course through the character, and they inform the moment. You let the moment inform the character using the new setting as inspiration for new feelings, or as a canvas on which to paint the new (or heretofore unrealized) feelings.

The cast members who are not in the scene follow to observe the scene, or they quietly fade out to run ahead to the location that they have chosen for the next scene so as to be prepared to begin it right away. The one guideline is that an actor instructs the director as to where the next scene is going to be. For the scene that is going to happen next, the actors need to choose who will stay behind and lead the group and the director to the site. Often, this is an easy choice; it is usually an actor whose character enters a bit later in the scene. It can also be the actor who begins a scene—leading to a more seamless start for the company. Surrounding the magical, creative choices of the paratheatric run with practical, cool-headed help like this is important. The relay is done in a timely fashion, of course, as the paratheatric run progresses.

The director's job, then, is to write down entirely positive notes. Not "positive" in the sense of pure praise but "positive" in the sense of noting when and insofar as possible what aspects of the run newly informed the scenes in a way that should be kept in the performance. This can be new stage movement, or new acting choices, or experiences that should be remembered to great impact on the performance.

Earlier, the blazing exercise determined which areas of the paratheatric space are useable and safe. Any and all of these are ripe for exploration by the cast as a part of the paratheatric run. I have found that each site—from suburban mansion and adjacent grounds to rural farm or beach by the sea—has something to offer the creative collective that forms around and for this technique.

There is a flow to the paratheatric run, and a true sense of storytelling that needs to be emphasized. The actors who bring the group to the next scene see their work directly impacting the next scene. Like juggling, it is very strenuous work that produces a clear flow, an almost effortless appearance. The cast will feel it when it happens, and will work to help it along.

Your attention as the director is crucial—you must summon every ounce of your concentration to be totally present for each and every moment of the paratheatric run. I have found that this attention is similar to the attention one needs in regular rehearsal, especially improvisational work. It brings you back to that place where the play really is everything in the whole world. This is the line of flow the performance is supposed to invite the audience toward; having the cast there first is probably the most essential element of theatre of any kind, anywhere.

The paratheatric run is, perhaps, similar to certain therapeutic techniques at first glance. The group cohesion that results from meeting the challenges inherent in the form cannot be denied. However, its primary purpose is artistic, and the selective role of the director would be ignored at great peril to the work, just as ignoring the injunction against drugs and alcohol would be destructive. Personalities shine in a few days of concentrated effort like this, and solitude can be found in the nourishing setting of fellowship around the work.

Aesthetic truths found in the rehearsal room, and in the outdoor exercises of the day before, inform the paratheatric run. The relationships created between the characters become tested and thereby strengthened by their portrayal in a new and multidimensional milieu. The flow and interplay of generation and selection that is behind so much good, deep theatre is no more evident than it is in the paratheatric run and in its impact on the performance run of a play. It is in this sense some of the most purely artistic work that our varied and collaborative, chaotic, and wooly art form presents.

As rigorous as it is, the paratheatric run is art for the artist's sake. It is not for the audience's sake, because the audience is not present. The actors who watch the work contribute to the creation of the informative experiences in a way that begins to train the whole cast (and director, if he is paying attention). So, in the theatre, art for artists' sake is called rehearsal, not performance, and it has its own beauties for the initiated. It is practice, in the very best, "do-ing" sense of the word. The paratheatric rehearsal, run, and resulting theories and ideas are meant to take this fact and explore it in a new way for gorilla theatre. It provides richness and durability to the choices actors make.

To review, your paratheatric run will need adequate time, and your cast adequate rest, to accomplish. Here is a tip that I have used in guiding casts: cheat. When it comes to the pure form, the scene-to-scene remodeling of the production, some caucusing may be in order. I remind the cast of this when I feel that they are unnecessarily intimidated by the austerity of the form—and it hasn't hurt when I did it. At meals the day before, or during a break, the scene-groups meet and come to a consensus as to the location to try for their scene.

Weaving the work over the site, from place to place and scene to scene, is a real articulation of all the previous work, and it allows new discoveries, which have been boiling beneath the surface, to work. Remember that nothing is going to transform a bad actor into a good actor. Talent is the beginning. The paratheatric run allows a moving, dynamic, and yet, at this stage, actor-controlled milieu for the talent, sincerity, and detailed characterizations of the participants to contribute to the strength and distinction of the gorilla-theatre aesthetic.

The sense of scale that many of the previous day's exercises have meant to instill is crucial, although by no means indiscriminately applied. The softest whisper, said with the intent and magic of the art form, can carry across to audience members fifty yards away. This kind of magic is one of the things that we hope to invite with the paratheatric run.

Directions for paratheatric run are summarized here:

1. For each scene, the actors will reach consensus as quickly as possible as to where within the boundaries of the paratheatric run the scene will take place.
2. The entire cast will move from place to place with the scenes, with the sole exception of the actors in the next scene, who might slip away to get to the new area—leaving one behind to guide the rest (and the director, who will guide the videographer if there is one).
3. At the conclusion of the run, the group will come together for warm-down, and won't discuss the work directly with each other for a period of three days. Time will be allowed for the actors to write in their notebooks about the work before the next meal.
4. After the run and warm-down, the work will be brought exactly into the performance in many ways. In terms of actual blocking

changes and interpretive changes, the director's notes will provide the tools for importing whatever will improve the performance.

Examples of Staging Brought Back

I could provide numerous examples of staging brought back into gorilla-theatre performance, but I will limit it so as not to stifle your own discoveries. The first one I always think of as "The Fool on the Hill."

In *King Lear*, the famous scene in which Lear rages against the elements has become an emblem for the entire theme of the play. It is never the easiest play to direct, if you are taking it seriously, and it presents many challenges. But telling that story well is so satisfying that it is worth doing your very best to be up to the test. I had been blessed with a wonderful cast of actors who were doing well and working hard right up to the paratheatric rehearsal we had planned. The one bugbear that I had left was how to stage the storm scene. Or, more specifically, how to portray the storm. Giant fans and water jets soaking the audience? Well, they might not hear King Lear, and that would be a mistake—especially with the Lear we had cast. Traditional thunder-sheets hung from the nearby trees? Silly. And potentially scene-stealing in a bad way. I had visions of mylar ribbons, balloons, and at one point soap-bubble machines, but no matter how I turned it, it wasn't right "in the tank" (as I sometimes call my imagination).

As the paratheatric run began, I let the picayune cares fall away and devoted my full attention to the work at hand. And it was fiery and wonderful. Cornwall paced toward Gloucester as he was about to blind him, banging a hammer along an old beam in the barn we were in to punctuate each terrifying question, while his wife grinned. There was some of the actor's joy of discovery in that grin, but it came off chillingly. More and more, each scene seemed to outdo the next for creativity and pure joy in the storytelling. Before we knew it, we were at the storm scene. I ran through a break of tall trees, out into a field, took a left, and followed Lear up to a small, abrupt hillock that was completely covered in yellow flowers, all about waist high.

As I looked up in amazement at Lear against the tall, tall sky, my bones shook and my skin crawled as his voice echoed off the valley surrounding us. The actor picked up the inspiration of it and really made the character sing, not literally but in the working of the words, with no self-indulgence and with a kind of ringing, self-evident truth, tragedy, and beauty. And he did all of this, despite the obviously bright, sunny day in the midst of the most unbearable storm that raged and raged. Was it really there? No, but I was there, made to be there by the Fool, who, with incredible physical acting intensity, was slowly being rolled up and down and back and forth on the hill by unseen gale force winds that he struggled against. What an incredible counterpoint to Lear's speech! The two of them told the literal tale and the symbolical truth of the effects of the king on the world—and of the world on the king—right there in a meadow in upstate New York. It was incredible, and it solved my problem of the storm quite neatly. The site where we had the gorilla-theatre performance of *Lear*, Washington Square Park, in those days had a trio of hills that seemed custom-made for gorilla shows. I put Lear on top of one of them, fired up some lights, and let the Fool do his magic reaction to the storm. I had painted a dashed line around the hill, and the audiences cooperated fully in the creation of the moment.

Writing about that year's *A Midsummer Night's Dream* paratheatric rehearsal that she had observed for the *Village Voice*, Francine Russo gave this opinion in her article:

> Is there something to this paratheatric preparation? In the performances in Washington Square, Demetrius did indeed look agitatedly around as he warded off Hermia's attentions. And, when Hermia stepped into the flat, grassy area where the four meet in the "woods" she bent as if ducking under bough and lifted her feet as if stepping over rocks and fallen branches. More than such physical gestures, though, the wild spirit of the fairies overrunning their hills and glades infused this delightful performance, and the lovers seemed truly confounded by their magic. . . . On the practical side, the cast successfully projected the poetry over great distances, airplane buzzing, shouts, and sirens. They seemed completely at home with the text and conveyed its meaning to the appreciative crowd, who pursued them good-humoredly as they sprinted . . . from jungle gym to asphalt hill to trampled grass clearing.

When rehearsing for the first year of *Macbeth* at Fort Tryon Park, very early in the play the actor playing Macbeth took us to the front lawn of the palatial house where we were guests. It was an extraordinary opportunity—the hosts had already moved into an even more palatial and grand estate across town, and this one was empty. It lay waiting for our imaginations to fill it. To be sure, I was surprised that the actors used the interior of the house so much—I had expected to be running through the adjacent hills and forest more. However, the paradigm was made clear by Macbeth in one moment on the lawn. As he walked back and forth, preparing to enter the scene in the front yard, he looked at the house, and he wanted it. Everything that he desired was knit up in that house, and I could see it in his eyes. This proved to be a lynchpin in his character's arc that day; as he became more and more isolated, he became more and more trapped in that house. The grand, sweeping room of the banquet scene became the tiny, closetlike attic room that he ended up in, raving at fate and vowing to fight to the end.

This was the same location where in *Twelfth Night* the duke's servant called to the duke "will you go hunt, my lord?" This was in the adjacent woods, though, and the exasperation in his voice was palpable. We kept it in for the performance, of course.

The physical cues that the paratheatric rehearsal builds into the actor's body will recall the new emotional worlds that are evoked. All of the tools actors learn in their technique classes can be used to mine the work here for substance. You, the director, must keep an eye out for the new form that it takes. Whole casts are made up of trained and experienced actors, each conversant in a different idiom of actor training, but they all come together in the paratheatric rehearsal process to forge the aesthetically complex but consistent interpretation that gorilla theatre needs in order to thrive.

Integrating Paratheatric Discoveries

After a day of rest following the paratheatric run, it is time to get to work brushing up the show using the discoveries of the last few days. Much of this work will take care of itself, or be looked to by the actors, after the reinforcement of the notes. Still, time needs to be devoted to specifically working in the blocking changes. The temptation at this stage is usually to push too hard for performance quality on the first reblocking attempt.

Instead, the quality of the work needs to be recalled carefully as the actor slowly walks through the new patterns. At first, a self-narration is often useful. Each actor helps describe the change and how it happened, when the existing blocking was used, and when the new variation came in. It is much like the bonfire tale-telling exercise, but with the addition

Inside acting: Jy Murphy and Lynda Kennedy in *Sailing to Byzantium*. Photo by Elliot Deal.

of the actors carefully walking through the play, adding more and more detail each time, until the thing runs itself. It is your job as the director to point out what needs to be done to the very best of your ability. And it is their job to do it, which is a whole different thing, and they need you, at times like this, to step back and allow the work to develop.

A favorite children's book of mine is called *Frederick the Mouse*, or maybe just *Frederick*. It tells the story of a mouse who, all summer, watched his fellows store away grain for the winter. He sat around, and they wondered what he could be doing. Then, deep in the winter, as the mice sat in their bare hole, well fed but bored by the dullness of winter, Frederick spun visions of the summer colors and feelings, evoking happier times for the mice. I seem to remember that they realized what he had been doing and said in their surprise something to the effect of "Oh, Frederick! You're a poet!" If only artists were as appreciated by men as they are by mice . . . Still, it is your job as the director to remind the actors of the feelings and give them your specific impressions of what worked well just enough to set off their own re-creation of it in the milieu of the gorilla production.

You will need at least one dress run of the show before you open it using the gorilla-theater technique. It is the hardest run. The actors are taking so much energy and discovery out to a partner who is missing—the audience. Still, this pain makes it all the sweeter to have an audience to work with. In the case of a last-minute staging, as when you are touring and the schedule goes wrong, or when you have had the dress run and then opening night rains out, you may need to use a "mark-through." This is essentially just a speed-through of the lines, with the actors moving through the blocking quickly to remind themselves. It is like talking to themselves, but together, and it takes less of the precious energy needed for performance. This is why a mark-through is often the best course of action on an afternoon when, after a late arrival, you will have to perform in a new site.

Variations and How to Invent New Paratheatric Rehearsal Procedures

When looking for sites for your paratheatric rehearsal, remember the scouting of locations for your gorilla-theatre production. For our production of *Sailing to Byzantium*, Gorilla Rep launched the rehearsal process with a paratheatric, and this was appropriate for the stylized production. We went to the sea, where we were lucky enough to have had a site donated, and we explored the author's obsessions with the notions of the sea with new exercises and physical meditations on the production's themes.

You can keep an eye out for paratheatric rehearsal sites as you build your image file and design the production, and as you travel around investigating the world. I haven't found a way to pay for it yet, but Arthur's Seat in Edinburgh, Scotland, would make a fantastic site for these experiments with any number of gorilla productions. The work could be staged right there later, and it is one venue that the famous Edinburgh Festival and Fringe hasn't explored, as far as I know. You take the high road, and I'll take the low road, and you can build your paratheatric rehearsal process and gorilla-theatre production in Edinburgh if you get there before me! Just make sure it is a good one—I would hate to be said to have inspired mediocrity. *Macbeth* naturally comes to mind as well suited to the space, but there are even better and more fitting shows to be done and rehearsed at Arthur's Seat.

To invent new paratheatric rehearsal notions, you will have to be inspired by the text you are working with and ask yourself where they might come to life from the mundane concerns of everyday life. Some have created interior retreats called "lock-ins," and interior paratheatric ideas like that might prove fruitful. I once asked a company to bring me and a cast of actors along on a six-month rotation to their South Pole operation to build a few shows, but they were short on space for their workers as it was. The "beehive" group improvisation that Andre Gregory talks about in the film *My Dinner with Andre* could almost be shaped into a rehearsal process, but it would need the differentiation of actual sculpting toward performance.

Think of a location that inspires you, even if it is an ordinary farm. As I say, it is the imagination that needs natural shapes and environs to open up into. Look at what you have available and never stop asking that might be possible there, and who might be able to help you achieve it. I have wanted to take a cast to Iceland to rehearse *King Lear* ever since I heard about Kevin Kuhlke's workshops there, and I have asked about it from time to time with donors, sponsors, and even folks who have houses and land there. It hasn't happened yet, but I won't stop asking.

For years, I have had a complete paratheatric rehearsal process and staging notes prepared for use aboard the space shuttle, and a theatre designed to fit onto it or on the international space station that is being built. NASA hasn't returned my e-mails or letters to date, but would you help get my cast of *Midsummer Night's Dream* up into space? The three-dimensional mobility is an ideal metaphor for the fairies' movement, and the staging notes alone, should they deliver a good show, might point the way for new ideas of human motion in zero gravity.

It is the artists moving into a neighborhood that always help turn it around and make it popular. So, I ask you again, can you help get my cast and me into space for a truly revolutionary experience of *A Midsummer Night's Dream*? I can double-cast it down to twelve mission specialists (actors) in addition to me and a technical assistant/documentarian. Too many deep sacrifices have been made by too many people to let our culture stifle and retreat from the dream of civilization in space. My dream for that civilization is that it should have theatre from its very infancy.

chapter **seven**

On-Site Directing and Operational Practices

Practicing Nonconfrontational Conflict Resolution

The best way to enter into any negotiation is to think of what you can give. In a confrontation with an unruly audience member during a public performance, a negotiation takes place. If the disturbance is large enough to warrant calling "cut," then you are negotiating for the continuance of your performance and the level of quality that your dedicated audience deserves. So, what can you give the person? Their dignity, for one thing. Most people respond well to being treated with respect. I won't make this a lesson that is better taught by Dale Carnegie, but being respectful and rephrasing as questions what you might feel are reasonable demands will go a long way.

I have found that when more than one person is involved in the disturbance, things get harder. Not impossible, but the situation needs more delicate handling. Still, persistence and integrity will usually win out. When the person is on drugs, as will happen in inner-city parks, you just have to call the police and wait. Never, ever, under any circumstance, should an actor or crew member handle a heckler directly. In performance, of course, it is different—a little ad-lib give and take can do the trick, or even lines taken directly to the audience member—but after "cut" is called, the roles change.

Also, when the disturbing party mentions violence, the negotiation is over. Once your troublemaker talks about violence, stop talking to them, call the authorities, and try to stay connected to your audience if possible. Letting them know what is going on as it is going on will help you resume the show when you are ready.

If, or course, threats of violence include the appearance of a weapon (this has never happened in any of my productions), common sense demands that the actors, audience, and crew leave the area in all haste.

Cut Procedure

During a gorilla-theatre performance, any member of the cast or crew is free to call "cut!" any time. Based on an idea that I learned from Richard Schechner, the practices regarding this have come to be called *cut procedure* around Gorilla Rep. I ask the cast or crew to stop the performance if anything is making them worry more about their safety than about the character or the show they are working on. From the time they call "cut" until the time I call "action," I have the job of trying to clear up whatever the problem is.

All actors and crew are asked to drop character, or drop what they are doing, and pay attention to the person who has called "cut." Often, this somewhat disturbing sight is enough to stop the disturbance. As I assure those who haven't seen the procedure at work, when actors drop character, it is as obvious (or more so) as if they had dropped their pants. The audience knows a lot, and (as in many cases) we should give them credit for it.

Now, the usual garden-variety "cut" is on account of a little heckling getting out of hand. In this case, the first thing I do is to try to bring some humor into the crisis situation. "Hey! We had auditions. Where were you?!" usually gets a laugh. In fact, it usually gets the heckler to peer out of his beer-fog long enough to realize that he wasn't just messing up the show for the actor to whom he was cat-calling, but that a whole audience is waiting for him to stop and go away. Usually, the hecklers hastily apologize and move off. Sometimes, they stick around and enjoy the show.

If your disturbance is more belligerent, you have to try a little negotiation. In most cases, hearing them out for a moment and treating them respectfully will clear things up. Other times, you have to be ready to call the police. I make sure a crew member is ready to do this at all times. As I tell the actors, if they hear me calling for the police, I am under no circumstances bluffing. For me, the key in these situations is never to bluff. If you say, "I'm going to call the police if . . ." and the "if" occurs, you have to call the police immediately to maintain any credibility. On the rare occasion that things have gone this far, the sight of friendly police officers on the way has usually caused the troublemaker to take flight.

Because you will have forewarned the local constabulary of your presence in the park, they will usually be on the alert. NYPD beat cops have made it a habit to drop by our performances. A well-placed call for a round of applause during the curtain speech for the folks in blue never hurts.

What I have seen during cut procedure is a lot of gorilla casts taking responsibility for the quality of the work. My usual speech continues with an appeal to the audience, such as "We care about the quality of what we are giving you. With this disturbance going on, that is not what you are getting, so we appreciate your patience while we wait until it passes." With the crowd on your side, the disturbance will usually go right away.

The Role of the Director in Performance

DIRECTING THE AUDIENCE

In my experience with Gorilla Rep, the role of the director in perform- ance has been crucial. No one likes to be caught off guard by pretentious experiments, and a director's note in a program does little to warm up the audience to what you are doing. You need to address the audience directly, at the top of the show. Stay connected with the audience and actors by closely observing their interaction during the performance.

Ellen Stewart, legendary producer of La Mama E.T.C. in New York, always framed her shows with a brief speech. After ringing her trademark hand bell, she'd let you know why you were there and what was so spe- cial about what you were about to see.

At a gorilla-theatre show, the director needs to step out and transi- tion the audience into what they are about to see *and* do. He or she is one part carnival barker, one part ringmaster, and a bit of a salesman. Your enthusiasm will be catching, and your speed, clarity, and energy will set the tone for the actors. Here's the text of my speech, which I modify as needed:

Hello, and welcome to our production of *A Midsummer Night's Dream*! My name is Christopher Carter Sanderson. I directed the show and I'd like to tell you a few things about the show that I hope will increase your enjoy- ment of it. It is a gorilla-theatre show, which means we will be moving from place to place as we go from scene to scene! We invite you to move with us as we go—we only ask that if you are the first folks on the scene that you please sit down so that others behind you can see. If you should not be able to see and hear to your complete satisfaction at all times, please don't hesitate to move as well! Watch out for the wires as you go, and when in doubt go right up behind the lights or to the edges of the light pools on the scenes and have a seat. We never pause or hesitate between scenes! We feel it would be condescending and therefore eschew it! The last line of any scene is the cue line for the next scene, so remember: a little hustle will always get you a front-row seat! We are Gorilla Rep, and this is *A Midsummer Night's Dream*!

Although that's not the playwright's version of what I say about all this, it is a true copy of what has been working for audiences over Gorilla Rep's many fruitful years. This speech introduces you as the one who is responsible. And, although you can't always make things go right as the director you often can. A smile and a pointing finger in response to a audience member's quizzical face during a scene shift can help speed an easier transition into understanding how this all works for that audience.

At the conclusion of the performance, I give another brief speech, this time with a bucket in my hand. From across the footlights (or work-lights, or flashlights, or what have you), I deliver "the ask," as salesmen call it, for an on-the-spot donation. Do you long, as a director, to know if the crowd has really enjoyed the show? Let me tell you, when a cloud of hands holding dollar bills arises out of a sea of smiling faces, you know one thing for sure: they liked it. Here's the text, more or less, that I've used with Gorilla Rep:

Thanks, folks! You've been a wonderful audience! [If cheering warrants it, it is time to say, "Shall I bring them back?!" And grin through as many curtain calls as are necessary. Longtime gorilla Greg Petroff will probably correct me on this, but I think ten is the Gorilla Rep record. Never force a curtain call and, when in doubt, go on with your speech.] Again, thanks! Believe it or not, folks, it takes money to make free theatre! We've got to find costumes, rent rehearsal space, pay the actors something, and copy programs. So, I'd like you to think about the value of the entertainment you received tonight. I hope it was at least equal to that of a film . . . or a Broadway play! Think about how much you might have paid for that and consider dropping a donation in the bucket here. We take checks, and your check is tax deductible to the maximum extent allowed by law, as we are a registered not-for-profit. We take plastic—just drop it in and I'll get it back to you! [Laughs, usually.] We are Gorilla Rep! Goodnight! [Take a quick bow and approach the first outstretched hand with the bucket held high.]

Although it would seem to be counter to conventional wisdom, I believe that these spontaneous cash flows do not in fact hamper the longer-range and larger-scope fund-raising efforts of the theatre company. I think that those who give more by check and via the mail or Web site still like to throw in a bit at show's end to show that they enjoyed it— and others who are more spontaneous will give what they are going to there or forget about it anyway. My experience is that people have an attitude toward this kind of giving that is similar to their attitude when tipping. The real bill for the meal is paid by the annual fund-raising drive, and the site donations at shows are the tip. In addition, the donation hat at the end allows those who can't afford to give much to do so in comfortable anonymity.

The director leads by example in the performance, in a way, so his or her attitude will help guide the audience's experience—as much as anything other than the acting can. As a plane flies overhead making a discernable noise, an audience member might glance at you to see if you are going to call "cut." Your locked focus on the acting will help guide them back to the action as well. An activated audience will often buttonhole you afterward for tips on the style, or to guess at what cuts you made in the text to provide such a sleek running time. Of course, you made no cuts, and the pace, coupled with the intense concern for detail, is what carried the work along so quickly.

Directing the Actors

Directing during the show, in short and precise doses, can enhance the work for some actors. At some point, it is important to ask the cast if they would like to try this, or let them know it is available if needed. Even something as simple as your pair of eyes can be helpful in this dynamic situation. When an actor circles by the electrics control area to check with you about a choice or correction that they worked on in a preceding scene, you generally know that they have become engaged in crafting a specific experience for that particular performance's audience. A lot of this kind of directing is coaching, giving brief encouragement or impressions of the audience's "feel."

Actors will benefit from feedback during the performance. The chief form of this feedback is from the audience, of course. As they run from scene to scene, smiling and working with the story, the actors can feel it. If they need a brief word of affirmation, give it to them if it is possible. Even a smile and a thumbs-up works wonders, especially if the audience is much larger than what the actor is used to. In the overrun situations, where hundreds of audience members exceed what would seem to be the capacity of the space and the work, the actors and I just smile and shake our heads at each other, as the audiences stay and stay and won't leave the scene, even after multiple curtain calls. Find a way to keep connected to the actors like this. It improves the performance in many ways.

One way that helps is by taking notes as much as you can during the performance. I make these kinds of notes available to actors at their discretion after the show is on its way, except when something is truly out of line and needs to be addressed immediately, though that has happened very rarely. More often, the notes specify ways for the actor to apply the early improvisation work in the performance, or they contain specific line details that might be of value to think about. I carry a small notebook and pen in a pocket or beside the light switches if that's my duty station, and I jot down notes as the show goes on. Each actor will access them as he or she is ready. As each actor is different, some prefer an e-mail with a summary, others a brief chat before the show. As I have often said, the best note right after a show is "congratulations!" Performance notes should come either just before performance, when they can be useful, or whenever the actor is ready.

NEGOTIATING THE SITE

Your stage manager will be seeing to running the lights, and your actors might be setting their own props, but someone's got to keep an eye out for the overall quality of the evening's performance. And that someone is the director on site. In a dynamic environment, a hand on a light that's fallen out of focus, or a quiet word to a group of people who are walking by with a loud radio can help keep things a little more comfortable for everyone. As the police patrol walks by, it is a good opportunity to explain what is going on. After all, people looking for your show will be asking them for directions!

Jy Murphy as the White Rabbit in *Alice in Wonderland*, Federal Plaza, New York City, 1997. Photo by Benjamin Heller.

I have always found it to be of great value to have a stack of promotional cards on site in addition to the show's programs. This is not "street theatre," because there is a committed group of folks who show up to see the show and not just passersby. The spectacle of several hundred people running around in pursuit of a cast of strange characters can be diverting indeed to folks just out for stroll. About Gorilla Rep's *Alice in Wonderland*, Anita Gates wrote in the *New York Times*:

> Alice in Wonderland, the way Gorilla Repertory Theatre Company does
> it, would be great to happen upon while strolling down Lafayette Street at
> twilight. Look, Ethel, there are some crazy people in funny hats and wigs
> running around outside that office building. And some other people keep
> following them every time they move from one group of park benches to
> the other. Let's check it out.

Sometimes, passersby are on the way to a party or are walking the dog, and a well-timed flyer or promotional card brings them right back the next night—with friends in tow.

Dynamic directing, or directing in performance, has much impact on this performance style. I think that until the work is really living in the world, a director on site will be needed just to help people learn how to handle themselves quickly, using subtle cues. Often, the mere act of running hard from scene to scene, being the first one in the first row in every place shift, can inspire an audience to follow suit and learn quickly that this improves their experience. I always have an assistant perform this task when I have other duties to perform. We call this position "the runner," and it goes well with signaling duties when some of the light cues need a signal from near the action.

When you are using powerful flashlights to light your show instead of stationary groups of lighting instruments, the director needs to be the most disciplined member of the team with the flashlight. Wandering attention means lagging lighting with this technique, and you can't afford to let your attention wander for a moment. Perhaps one of the most imitated of my techniques, after the gorilla staging itself, the flashlight technique can just as easily backfire. Just as a gorilla show that adds long pauses between scenes is bound to be long and boring, and probably fail, so sloppy flashlight use will cause audiences to lose focus. I discuss this more in chapter 10, but remember that just as the director must be the most disciplined person in the rehearsal room, he or she must also be the quickest and the most disciplined with the flashlight scene after scene.

Be ready for the happy accident, of course, but also prepare yourself for as many eventualities as might reasonably occur. I carry the following things in my pockets during all performances: aspirin, band-aids, Krazy Glue, a Swiss Army knife, and strips of gaffer's tape. May your crew be large and able, but be ready to help them when you are needed. It is a good example to set if you can.

PREPARE AND TRAIN

A director preparing for work on site is, on a fundamental level, doing the same thing actors do to prepare: rehearsing. In the early days of this style, I would role play with the actors and improvise a few cut-procedure scenarios, just to make them feel comfortable. You pick the roles, talk through the scenario all the way to the end, and then act it out. After a few humorous attempts, insist that it be played straight a few times, and everyone will benefit by getting a clearer idea of what is expected of them.

It goes without saying that your beginning and ending speeches should be memorized and rehearsed, so that you feel comfortable with them. You can also learn a lot about how to handle yourself on site by expanding your idea of what constitutes influence over the spectacle a bit. Watch your favorite sports coach. During an important game especially, you will see that a cool, calm, patient coach inspires a team—and an audience—with confidence in a way that no hothead will ever be able to. For example, Manager Joe Torre of the New York Yankees demonstrates directing on site that is truly inspiring.

Now, a baseball manager wears a uniform like a player, and I have found that, depending on the show, a director who wears a kind of uniform can be more effective. Over the years, I have experimented with wearing things in keeping with the theme of the show's costumes, and I've tried white tie and tails, regular suits, and the all-black ensemble of a technician. Each was, I think, appropriate to a particular show and a particular audience's geist, or spirit, at a particular time. In the end, directing on site is an art, and you have to make the artistic decision that works for you. I have noticed that people seem to donate a bit more to the hat at the end if I am wearing a tie, but because the dust and the work of setting up and tearing down make wearing a tie uncomfortable and rumples it up, I have not worn one much over the years. For a while, with the comedies, a really large, funny hat was the thing. When audiences began stuffing the hat over-full at the end of the shows, I carried a box.

Teaching is a natural extension of the role of the director in a gorilla performance. With the high school groups that have visited us, a brief talk and a question period after shows has always gone very well. If you have the chance to teach workshops as a director outside of your gorilla experience, learning to address classes well will help you develop a style to use in performance. Certainly, the open, interactive nature of good teaching will bring its spirit to your work.

The best training is the doing. Paying close attention will teach you what you need to do as you work to facilitate the union of audience and cast in performance. Keep an eye out for ways to facilitate each perform-ance, and make notes about what could have gone better.

chapter eight

Organizational Approaches

Mission Statement and Incorporation

There are plenty of great books about running a not-for-profit organization. Among the best is *The Nonprofit Entrepreneur* (1988) by Edward Skloot. What I have found is that a properly phrased mission statement informs every action of a theatre company with a clear sense of purpose. Often, the best response to a question, especially the question "Why?" is to quote a good mission statement. For outdoor, environmental gorilla theatre, this is crucial to the survival of the company from show to show. The form demands different resources and a different set of needs, and these should be clearly dictated by a clear set of values. All of this is old news—just make sure those values are clearly and specifically defined in your mission statement if you incorporate as a not-for-profit. Many for-profit ventures have profited from having a good mission statement as well, because they work.

Again, Gorilla Repertory Theatre Company NYC, Inc.'s mission statement:

> Gorilla Repertory Theatre Company, Inc.'s mission is to provide the highest quality productions of classical dramatic material, with the flavor of contemporary immediacy, for people where they are, and free of charge to them.

The gorilla aesthetic serves this mission. There is a populist truth inherent in the gorilla style and, although it can be built in a for-pay setting, it has its true roots in an open audience. I had been working on *A Midsummer Night's Dream* and the first two Gorilla Rep seasons before the mission was distilled. It was invented by the board to best express the essential motivation behind the work we were doing.

We spent a weekend under expert guidance of a consultant in this area who volunteered her time to help us put together the statement. Her process helped us to zero in on specific words that felt right through the course of a specific program. In the end, we could all agree that this was a mission statement that the company had been serving and should continue to serve. We inserted "for free" several years later, even though our work in the parks had always been free of charge. It was the best way to serve the mission, but, because it was hard to explain to some people initially, we made it a part of the mission statement to make the principle clear as a value of the company.

On Broadway, every new production is spun off as a separate corporate entity by its producing entity. Although each of your gorilla shows will have its own spreadsheet in the record books, there will be a unifying aesthetic that your audience comes to rely on. No show of yours will earn a silly nickname like "The Very Slow Wives of Windsor" among your actors. The directing of the show itself is made easier by the clarity of thought that it takes to make a good, simple mission that you can stick to. If you can't, chances are your thinking is all over the place and needs to get sorted out. A company making gorilla theatre makes a name for itself, and that name is a brand that has meaning. Keeping the mission statement clear helps make that meaning specific, show after show.

Working with Volunteers

You may have a fully funded organization that does not require volunteer aid. However, I found that, over the years, we have relied on volunteers to help. Well-defined tasks, clearly broken down into steps that can be accomplished by more than one person in series, are an important part of making sure your volunteers are happy and comfortable. Everyone likes to help out with gorilla shows, and they are fun to be around. If the tasks are broken down, they don't seem so overwhelming.

Recruiting volunteers to help with gorilla shows happens very naturally at the shows themselves. My first experience with volunteers was at the very first production of *A Midsummer Night's Dream* in Washington Square Park. Because we used flashlights to light the scenes as we went, it was clear that we could use help with that, and it also looked fun to do. We would give our new volunteers a T-shirt, ask them to wear black, and help them memorize the cues and technique for lighting. The only resistance I encountered was to the idea of lighting for the whole run—a long commitment of full weekends. So I simply asked the volunteers to coordinate their evenings, and this resulted in happy volunteers, none of whom was overworked, and a few extra lighters for each performance. This provided a model for gorilla shows and volunteer work as we went. Volunteers know how much time they can afford to donate, so let them have something to do that fits that time. Gorilla shows can always use an extra hand with programs or security.

The more responsibility the volunteers have, the more lengthy their qualifying period should be. In my experience, potential board members should be a part of the organization actively for about a year to guarantee that they were in the position for the right reasons. The board would allow the new member to have speaking privileges and to sit on committees, but full voting privileges would be withheld until the period was over and full membership ratified. Of course, we learned this the hard way.

Board officers are volunteers. They are special supporters, bringing fund-raising connections and organizational weight to your not-for-profit theatre company. The amount and kind of dedication that it takes to be a board member is hard to find. Sadly, people who like to exercise power for its own sake are not so hard to find. Clear job descriptions for the board and artistic director are very helpful. Essentially, the board has the selfless task of helping the artistic director accomplish the company's mission. This can get confusing because the board nominally hires the artistic director.

These days, most companies put a producer or managing director on a parallel position with the artistic director. This probably makes sense when a physical plant is part of the company's identity, and other activities occur there in addition to the direct mission-related artistic tasks. The compact, mobile nature of the gorilla-theatre style puts very different demands on the technical staff, and the organization should be flexible to accommodate these.

Volunteers with specific technical skills are especially valuable, and respect for their ability is mandatory. Whether it is cool design or a specific electrical task that needs accomplishing, a skilled volunteer can have a great effect in a very short period of time. Sometimes a skilled person needs a chance to demonstrate new abilities "for the résumé," but more often a senior, skilled worker will just want to chip in to help out this fun,

Alex Roe as Oberon in *A Midsummer Night's Dream* in Washington Square Park, August 1999. Photo by Benjamin Heller.

subversive style of theatre. I often ask audiences to drop their cards in the hat at the end if they would like to volunteer, and a card indicating that the person has specific skills is always a welcome sight.

The actors, when they are working for anything below scale, are volunteers too. They need to understand the conditions they will be working under so that expectations are appropriate to these conditions. I remember the first time I was able to provide a fourteen-cubic-foot truck on site for the actors to change in—there was a male and a female shift. Because we had made do without such a convenience for so long, I thought it was the height of comfort for the cast. Before, actors had worn their costumes to the site, or worn sweat clothes layered underneath to make changing easy. The director for whom I was producing had neglected to explain the way we work, and the actors complained to their union about it. We came up with a compromise, but it was at a cost. I can't remember a single actor with whom I worked, or who came to know the style, who complained in this way. And so this didn't have to happen. Careful explanation of how gorilla-style theatre works would have gone a long way to preventing the problem.

Gorilla theatre may also be the next phase of evolution of the position of artistic director. The latest trend in recent years has been to have the artistic director work as a director on at least a few shows in every company's season. Gorilla style may well benefit from small, well-organized companies whose entire oeuvre is directed by the artistic director. Rotating the position annually or semiannually might be another good alternative if the position remains a volunteer one. Good gorilla directors with a flair for pace and timing are hard to find, and worth building a company around.

The money that a board raises is used to fund both the eventual successes and failures of the company. It takes far-sighted individuals to see that both are necessary to an organization's growth. These successes and failures are perhaps more clearly seen as necessary in the growth of an individual artist. Gorilla Rep's board stayed small, with the advisory group growing and shrinking at different times over the years to accommodate different projects and goals. You can build a board that understands the needs of gorilla-style theatre; it just takes time, patience, and commitment on your part.

Interns

Interns can be a most valuable source of seasonal support and energy. Strictly speaking, an intern is a college student gaining credit and/or experience by working in an apprenticelike capacity. The key with gorilla interns is to give them responsibility not commensurate with their experience, but just beyond it. I have worked with interns in capacities as responsible as assistant director, even director, and had them rise to the occasion. There were no such opportunities for me (and in large part this may be why I was able to create my own distinct style). Making these opportunities happen has been part of what has kept up the energy at Gorilla Rep.

Internships are a direct way for gorilla-theatre groups on campus to communicate with extant groups in professional circumstances. Brown University's Shakespeare on the Green student gorilla-theatre group has sent many great interns to help with Gorilla Rep's work, and they took the tools and techniques they learned back to this thriving campus group.

The perspective that professional exposure brings to a student's work is not to be underestimated. My undergraduate work at New York University's Experimental Theatre Wing provided me with numerous opportunities. From banging bongos for howling performance artists at the Franklin Furnace, to playing the bass in *The White Whore and the Bit Player* at La Mama, to ushering at the Public whenever I had a chance, I grabbed these opportunities, and they helped me develop as an artist. Providing such opportunities is important to gorilla theatre and ensures its survival.

The workshops that I deliver around the country have been great contact points for intern recruiting as well. In general, though, I would say that interns need to experience a gorilla-style show before they contemplate helping out with the work. Again, the specific demands and rewards of the medium are clearest in its actual performance. Matching expectations to reality is easier when examples of that reality are readily at hand.

One important idea to keep in mind is the difference between an actor and an intern assistant. When I am approached by potential interns, I always ask them if they are asking to audition for me or asking for an internship opportunity. The student who wants to act in a gorilla-style show but is masquerading as an intern is rarely happy and is best advised to seek acting opportunities instead. Ivy League schools can be especially bad about supporting their budding professional actors at the undergraduate level, and therefore students from these schools should be most closely questioned.

On the other hand, a student who wants a closer look before auditioning or who knows they'll need more time to develop skills before they feel ready to perform should be encouraged to intern. Helping to make the work happen from the production side always makes better actors. It is a constructive energy to have around the work and encourages more experienced actors to pass along what they have learned in their gorilla work. Often, procedures can become so ingrained that they aren't thought about much, and a correct attitude is best taught by example. Gorilla theatre encourages a special kind of discipline.

Check with the intern's educational institution for exact reporting methods if the student is receiving credit for the work. This is often a one-page evaluation and can be easily completed if the student was doing real work.

Publicity: Homemade and Professional

My father, an advertising executive, still stands by the old wisdom that the only advertising worth anything is word of mouth. He warned me early in my career that throwing advertising money at a bad product wouldn't make it into a good product, and that a good product would sell itself. Fortunately, the energy of Gorilla Rep shows and unique gorilla-theatre style have always gotten people talking, and this has, in turn, led to bigger and bigger audiences. I believe that, after a quality show, the only thing you really need is listings—and perhaps a good review or two!

Although it is true that some publications will send along a reviewer only if you are purchasing advertising space, in the case of papers that have wider readership this is generally not true. People want to know where a gorilla show is happening and what it is like. Also, as it is a provocative aesthetic, critics generally seem to like the chance to weigh in with their opinions. Thankfully, those opinions have been largely on the positive side so far. Critics have a job to do, and hating them is an infantile indulgence that a professional theatre artist can ill afford. You will learn a lot from criticism that has integrity. Still, I do practice the old theatre tradition of not telling the cast that a critic is coming until after they have left.

A good example of critical integrity that taught me a lot happened early in Gorilla Rep's history. The *New York Times* critic Ben Brantley gave us our first *Times* review. It was for *A Midsummer Night's Dream* in Washington Square Park, in 1994, and it was included in the Critic's Notebook feature. It was a very good review and included things like:

a gymnastic, leather-lunged and tireless cast that keeps his 12 actors leaping, tumbling and dancing through the jungle gyms and roller skating hills of the parks playground . . . they actively work the audience, making brazen eye contact, grabbing onlookers by the shoulders and blithely shuffling them from site to site . . . the complicity between actors and audience is as genial and unforced as the theatre allows . . .

Great stuff, and good to remember during times of crisis, when the basics can be hard to focus on. Mr. Brantley was soon promoted, with much heralding, to the position of head critic. In a *Village Voice* interview soon thereafter, he noted that, although the pressures of his new job would compound with time, he would still be trying to get back to the small theatre companies who were doing work that interested him.

And he was as good as his word. The next season after his appointment, he came back to review Gorilla Rep's *King Lear*, also in Washington Square Park. The first night he came, we were treated to a torrential downpour halfway through the second act. As I scrambled to pack the spotlight and other gear, all I had time to get out was a quick, "Sorry, folks! Please come back on a dry night!" Of course, I wondered if he would come back—as a reviewer from *Time Out* magazine once neglected to do after being rained on. But he did come back the very next night; under clear, warm skies, he shuffled around with the rest of the audience. That review was, if possible, even more insightful and clear. I felt like someone really "got it."

One salient difference between the first production Mr. Brantley attended and the second was that, for the first, Gorilla Rep was handling its own press relations; by the second, we had secured the services of a good press representative. Press reps are important in the theatre, as everyone knows, because it is important to have someone a step away from the artistic process discussing it with editors. More so with gorilla theatre: you need a responsible professional to put the case to the press about what you are doing. More than that, you need someone who knows the lay of the land to help you put together a press plan. Reviews and coverage can happen by happy accident, or they can combine into a sum that is worth more than the total of its parts. Every once in a while, you get lucky enough to work with someone like the legendary Peter Cromarty who can mastermind such a plan. The key, as an artist, is to be ready when the luck comes.

In the meantime, as you are working up your publicity on your own, remember that no amount of coverage or spin is going to rescue a slow, boring show. It just isn't. The theatre profession might be a cynical one, even a jaded one, but it still falls in love with a great show when it sees one. Hundreds of audience members attending show after show and loving it creates a buzz that cannot lie. Corporate types will talk about "niche" and "demographics" until they are blue in the face, but success both defies and defines such ideas. Your professional telemetry creates the integrity that people want to be around. Press reps, the really good ones, can speak the language that editors understand and will explain this. If you don't have one, the shows will have to talk all by themselves. Assistants will come, there will be talk, and things will happen.

Keep in mind the two categories of your initial exposure to the press, and keep the efforts in both areas separate as well. These are, again, listings and reviews. The listings information go to the listings editors three weeks in advance. They contain bare-bones info, with spin kept to a minimum. The listings release says: here is what it is, here is when and where.

Read listings and get a feel for what they are looking for. The review release goes not to reviewers but to the editors who assign them. This should be less than one page, have some biographical information about the collaborators and artistic personnel, and talk about why the show is important or, better, fun. A third category of exposure exists, but it is harder to try without a press rep. This is the "story tip." Outside of New York City, it is a staple for most gorilla shows. In the story tip, you write the article you would like to see appear and send it to a few editors. From time to time, they like the idea, and a writer is assigned to put something together like it. This can lead to an interview, always a good draw when published. Readers like to see the person who was interviewed on the site, performing or directing. It is a good way to help people feel comfortable right away.

The way to sound good in an interview is simple: practice by going to parties. People will ask you what you do. Stay sober and practice answering in an interesting, coherent, and, *most of all*, brief manner. Let me say that again: in a brief manner. A sentence or two. If they are interested, short, punchy answers will do. Of course, good manners demand that you ask the same of them and listen to the entirety of their answers. This is as it should be. But I'll tell you: those short, punchy answers, and letting them lead as and where their interest in your gorilla exploits takes them, will come in handy on front of the camera and microphone. It's good practice. I have enjoyed being interviewed about the work, and topics and ideas brought to light in these interviews might provide food for thought in a prospective audience.

Another way to publicize your shows is to write articles yourself. These days, even the *New York Times* has people writing about their own work. Any local paper or Web site that would like some interesting content might run an article about your encounter with the gorilla-aesthetic movement. It breeds a host of anecdotes that people seem to find interesting, and a growing movement in the cultural world and specifically in the theatre generally merits interest in the media. I was lucky enough to write a print column for a few years, and later, as a guest editor for **theatremania.com**, I wrote a few interviews. When your byline sits next to a fun interview with an important and compelling figure, it does a good thing or two for your name.

In the end, getting the word out that a good gorilla show has turned up in an interesting place should take care of itself, with a little help from listings and reviews. If you have the budget and a mailing list, send out announcements; people still like getting well-designed postcards in their mailboxes. And if you take names from audiences, your mailings will be much more effective. I have never seen a group buy a list and be happy with it. Even hard-core theatregoers prefer to "discover" the gorilla aesthetic for themselves.

Sponsorship

Sponsorship is an uneasy subject, as the direct tit-for-tat of buying advertising space does not apply to gorilla shows. A merchant will have difficulty quantifying the return on his dollar donated. Still, it is not a dead issue, as these problems exist for all not-for-profit arts groups. Perhaps the best way to sell sponsorships is to point out that sponsoring a gorilla-style show is like sponsoring a little league softball team—except that entire families can play! Like most things, all good seems to come from the work itself. A sponsor needs to see a few hundred people running around enjoying themselves, and often they need to feel that they came up with the idea of sponsorship themselves. So invitations are appropriate, as are follow-up calls and notes. Longer, relationship-building strategies flourish around the good will generated by gorilla shows.

One of the organizations that sponsored Gorilla Rep early in its history sent their executive director to see a show. This was a few years into their sponsorship, and they had been giving about $500 per season fairly steadily. The show he came to see was *A Midsummer Night's Dream* in Washington Square Park. He didn't introduce himself at the beginning of the show but joined the group of people talking to me after the curtain speech. It was nice to meet him and to put a face to a name. But what was most fascinating was his reaction to the show. He was really flabbergasted, and almost at a loss for words. This from a very articulate corporate leader. Still, when he composed himself, he just wanted to say that he had seen the play countess times, but that this production had really drawn him into its world. He was frank about admitting that he had assumed that our attendance figures were a bit inflated, as apparently is the norm with sponsorship and grant applications.

It was a reaction similar to Hugh Hayes's, which was, if I remember correctly, something like, "I love *Midsummer* and have seen a million productions of it, but this time I felt like I was living in it!" He went on to quarterback the press-relations plan for that season, as he was working with its mastermind Peter Cromarty. Hugh is a sharp man, and a good one, and his attendance at a Gorilla Rep show really seemed to give him the extra spark that his genius needed to help us get on the map. Peter is a leader who trusts his people, and I'm sure he listened to Hugh's reaction and report.

Don't ever expect a slam-dunk to be a slam-dunk, and keep your eyes open for someone who really understands what you are doing with gorilla shows. None of the easy shots, the so-called no-brainers, ever worked in sponsorship pitches for Gorilla Rep. The power company donating a generator or an on-site hookup? It would seem clear, but it wasn't to the folks at the power company. Gorilla Rep doing a Nike ad, or at least getting a sponsorship for our well-loved and very athletic interpretations of classics? Nope. Brand managers are a hidebound bunch, and community outreach for them is a long-established program that does not include innovative theatre. The Gap, even after being mentioned in a *New York Times* review of a Gorilla Rep show, did not send a single T-shirt. This is not invective, gorillas, it is reportage for your benefit.

The most dangerous thing about sponsorship is, as with many fundraising ideas, that you cannot sell what is not for sale. People will try to steal the aesthetic and sell it, but it will not work. The perfectly rendered gorilla show, denuded of its in situ collaboration with the community, robbed of meaningful text to the point that it is clearly acceptable by corporate marketing departments, and cut to a television show's length, is no longer gorilla.

Logo banners placed nearby, product placement, and all of the traditional sponsorship plugs can work with gorilla-theatre shows, and they should be tried. Run any of these ideas by your local parks authority. The private company that runs Central Park for the New York City government is very stringent about enforcing the "no advertising" policy—to the extent that we're prohibited from writing arrows with chalk on the ground to direct people to the shows! Not even with the promise of washing off the chalk each night could they allow chalk signs pointing out how to get to our free shows. I'll leave it to you to figure out the local vagaries of where you are working; I can draw few coherent principles from the widely varying experiences that I have had trying to figure out sponsorship in free park shows.

The commissioner's offices and the individuals in higher positions in the Parks Department in New York have always been supportive. Embattled by underfunding, they have welcomed gorilla theatre as a way to enhance cultural offerings and bring people into parks for positive experiences. It may be that more coordinating naturally happens with better funding to the parks. Also, the more gorilla companies that form and distinguish themselves, the more they can go to government and parks representatives with a coherent plan for regulations and policies. In the meantime, sponsorship will be a case-by-case question. Don't compromise your program by not discussing this detail with your permit-granting entity.

Permits, Contracts, and Letters of Agreement

If "get it in writing" is rule number 1, then "carry a copy" is probably rule number 2. Things get confusing, and people get tired, so reviewing the written agreement of anything is necessary from time to time. It is not a sin, and it does not mean mistrust. If anything, I have found that a willingness to devote time and energy to clarifying things in writing has been a sign of professionalism.

A permit is a written agreement between you and the issuing authority, and it is worth carrying a copy of it on site at all times. Our brilliant production manager Big Willie made a habit of making copies of the permit and handing them out to me and the assistant director on site, just in case a question should arise. Production management should regularly file all legal documentation for review by anyone who wants to see it, especially if you are incorporated as a not-for-profit.

There is perception, there is reality, and there are the expectations. Expectations come in two kinds: realistic and unrealistic. The excitement that the theatre, our beloved art form, generates is undeniable. When this excitement is doubled by the gorilla-theatre style, the spotlight gets hot and unrealistic expectations can flare up. It is a source of dissonance for some to see hundreds of people in the audience but not a lot of money coming their way—and understandably so. However, when the show is being presented for free, huge paychecks or bonuses are an unrealistic expectation. When expectations get unrealistic, citing a written agreement becomes necessary. Taking the time to write them out and sign them will clarify what your wonderful gorilla show is and, more important, what it is not. A letter of agreement, or even a signed and dated memo will often prove to be an important reminder to all parties concerned.

Working with Designers

Design in the dynamic, gorilla outdoor environment means enhancement and reframing the mundane to transform it into the magical.

Design work turns out best if you are clear in your vision for the play and its impact on the audience. Working to communicate this design to the design staff early is important. For one thing, this will be a time when you are not under the pressures of an imminent opening of the production, Frankly, if a designer has a better idea, you'll be more likely to listen to it when there is time to think it over. What you see in your head for the show is good; it is rooted in what you want to say. Being open to better ways to say it is imperative. After all (again this is my father's advice), if you make an effort to and are able to surround yourself with talented people, why not listen to them? Of course you should, and the best way to help yourself do so is to get into design dialogue early.

Designers communicate visually, and so it is important to encourage them to clip pictures and to sketch; it is equally important that you share your image file with them and try to visually represent your ideas as clearly as you can. The designers are there to help you make your site come alive as a new world in which the story will happen, and clever design can truly transform a public space into the theatrical, dynamic setting that your gorilla show needs to be its best. Every visual element, or sound in the case of composers or sound designers, that is in the neighborhood of what you want communicates valuable information to the designers.

Referring to other works can seem counterintuitive at first, but it works. We are struggling to communicate a set of specific values, and examples always help. This was made most clear to me when communicating with the director of photography on a film project. He encouraged me to think about films that had the same visual "feel" as what I wanted. We ended up meeting once a week for a month or two and watching films together, using them as jumping-off points for discussion of our film. It made things so much more efficient when it came time to shoot that I applied the same technique when refining my communication with other designers, and it worked well. Even on the barest budget, a creative designer will enhance your gorilla work with their art.

A brief tune, rewritten to compliment the direction, can make all the difference in the world. "Hark, the Lark" in *Cymbeline* was an important moment in the Gorilla Rep Riverside Park production that went over well. Cloten is trying to impress Imogen with music, and yet, if the music was really impressive, it would undermine the inappropriateness of his suit. So I went over the top and wrote a little tuneful barbershop quartet number, drafting some of the actors playing other characters to hop in wearing boaters. It was simultaneously funny and out of whack, seemingly a witty diversion in Cloten's opinion, but wildly wrong for real wooing in Imogen's view. The audience got it, and laughed.

Keep a sharp eye out for unique design elements that will tell multiple stories at once and thereby effect this transition into magic. Your design team will be the source of many of these elements, and you can inspire them with others and with the transformative behavioral energy of the gorilla acting.

Working with an Assistant

To the date of this writing, I have never been an assistant director. That doesn't mean I think that it is a bad thing. In general, though, I do not agree with the statement that an assistant director is learning anything by sitting around all the time watching, with the occasional trip out for coffee. Again and again I will say it: the only way to learn to act is to act, and the only way to learn to direct is to direct. When I work with an assistant, I make sure they have work to do. If they are an assistant director, then they get to direct. That is the way is has to be to remain effective—any discussions (and there are no more fruitful artistic discussions than those with less experienced practitioners and junior colleagues) must be based on a real encounter with the work. Sitting around talking all the time leads to all kinds of bad stuff—jargonism, false understanding, and so on. An assistant needs to be actually doing some of the work. I hope that I have made that clear. You must make time to check over the assistant's work, of course, and if you can't bring yourself to commit to the work in this way, your gorilla theatre will suffer.

The ideal assistant relationship creates a growing feeling of responsibility and ability for the assistant, and a growing resource for you for getting work done. At a certain point, assistants have learned so well what is expected of them that, if they are about to fail or get into a situation that they can't handle yet, they know to ask about it. Feedback from the actors is important, and, especially at first, notes should not come directly from the assistant director. In time, the assistant director can go to the actors with notes, but this should be after checking them with you first.

This works best in brief meetings after a rehearsal slot, at first; eventually this can be accomplished in an e-mail or a quick phone chat. Later, your assistant understands your aims and something of your technique and can work more directly with the actors. The first step, I find, is well achieved by instructing the assistant director to organize line run-throughs and additional scene work outside of the rehearsal schedule. Later, as they are able, you can trust them with improvisation, work-through, or staging phases of scene work, and you can check their work in run-throughs.

A truly advanced assistant is one you would trust to finish directing the show if you were somehow incapacitated. This is someone, though perhaps a junior colleague, you would assist in executing a vision of theirs as well. This is an assistant who is ripe for a directing assignment of their own in your growing gorilla-theatre production company. They may start their own company or production, or work for other companies. I have found this an extremely effective way of bringing new directors to the aesthetic. There is no way to learn it but to do it, and pulling an indoor production apart and stringing it across a random landscape is not the way to do it. And that is precisely the risk of more seasoned directors jumping in—one that you can avoid by being aware of and building a growing, real world in your work.

Your assistants should be encouraged, if they are in school, to apply for academic credit for the work, and you will often need to provide a grade or evaluation. I think the work of writing up these evaluations is more than compensated for by the resource of a good assistant. The best way to write up grades that I have found is to be clear at the outset what the grading structure is, and then stick to it. The medium is fluid, and there are many challenges to be faced and discoveries to be made—in fact, there is room in the aesthetic for many points of view and separate styles. As the work progresses and makes its demands, the basic criterion for the grade should not change. I usually grade assistants and interns on reliability and tasks accomplished rather than improvement. That is, for instance, if the assignment has been to block a scene and it gets blocked, that part of the grade is accomplished—whether or not I have to rip the whole thing apart and redo it. Failure is, after all, an essential part of learning. This is a bit different from class grades, where in most instances the degree of improvement is part of the grade.

Working with Crews

The radical difference between volunteer and professional crews cannot be overstressed. My experience of them around gorilla shows has been mixed, and it breaks down pretty squarely in favor of the volunteers. I believe that this is because our organization has never had, to date, money to pay a proper professional crew and we have had to make do with the folks we could get at a substandard wage. Crew members who take a job because they see no choice and will do it until something better turns up are not the best crew members by definition—I wasn't a good crew member when I took such jobs right out of school. If you have to hire someone without the adequate resources, recommendations from people you know are going to be key. Even better is to call past volunteers and see if they would like to fill in for a while.

Once in place, a crew in the gorilla theatre needs training before deployment. After all, no matter how experienced they are in theatre tech, they probably haven't done a gorilla show, and they certainly haven't with you and this exact running crew. Actors changing costumes sometimes demand that a tent be set up, and other new demands create other new responsibilities; because these are new responsibilities that haven't been written about in the union rulebooks, they will need to be split up and taken care of ahead of time. The ideal is to leave the space looking like it did before it was theatricalized, so set-up and tear-down tend to be a little more radical than just taking out and putting away.

I have learned a number of things from watching independent and student film and video crews work, and the lighting set-ups on location have been instructive. Low-budget films have proven especially interesting, as the crews are small and ad hoc. Certainly, different habits and protocols exist between film and theatre crews, but there are lessons to be learned in both instances. The small film crew I worked with as a director was, I admit, surprised to see the director carrying lights and equipment around. Dividing up the crew into more specific set-up duties was a film idea that we used to set up Gorilla Rep shows very efficiently. The whole need to set up and transform a space and then take it back to the state it was in when you found it is a film-location commonplace. Although we have not yet managed to have a gorilla-theatre show site as well catered as a film shoot, we have adopted many practices over the years from observing them.

The concentration and discipline of the crew are a part of the setting. The audience observes their demeanor as a part of the show, even before it starts, and as it travels from place to place. You can consider it part of the frame if you wish but, in this sense, a sloppy frame will not set off your efforts well. Also, the focus and concentration that it takes to get a show moving from scene to scene as it moves around the park is well served by starting it before the audience arrives, and by continuing it as they arrive. It will help guide their focus on the work more surely than any follow-spot ever will.

If you have respect for the crew and their efforts, your crew will be more likely to respect your work and to show it in performance. They are as much a part of the show as the actors and the director. When good actors are a part of the crew for a gorilla show, they can learn valuable things about the skills required to pull it off well, and thereby they will be better candidates for roles in future projects.

As the show moves from scene to scene, the crew can often be at the edges of the audience's awareness, adding or subtracting from the focus. It bears repeating that there is no "offstage" in the classic, proscenium sense. As you walk through a museum and see a large painting with a gold frame, you know at least one thing: someone at some time thought that the painting was worth putting in such a frame. You know someone has cared about the painting, and this shapes your understanding of the painting; it influences it in an undeniable way. So can all of the details surrounding your gorilla theatre, most of all the attention and focus of a good crew.

Trucks and Trucking

As with any aspect of on-site production, truck use needs to be cleared with the permit-granting body. Whether all you need is a parking space, or whether you need to actually drive onto park land, the truck use needs to be approved. The park personnel know all the best ways to drive to your site anyway, so you may as well ask.

Over the years at Gorilla Rep, we have developed procedures that tend to make a truck on site unnecessary. The less heavy but equally bright photoflood lighting instruments can usually be broken down into a duffle bag or at most a hand truck. Actors don't seem to mind carrying a bag of props and costumes back and forth to the production.

Having a truck can bring unexpected problems, and you need to be prepared. I once made the mistake of parking in front of a poorly marked entrance to a very small alley. Although the alley was hidden, it was used by a woman who, I learned, frequently calls the police to tow away anyone parked over that patch. Even late at night when the unsuspecting driver who parked there is tired from working hard on a gorilla theatre show. Props, costumes, lights . . . all were stored safely, or so we thought, in the truck. A tip: lash everything down tightly and well. The truck was towed to the impounding yard and, if the gear had not been lashed down, it would have been tossed around in the back of that truck and broken beyond immediate repair. I did not have enough money in my bank account to pay the ticket, but fortunately one of the actors was able to lend the company the cash and meet me at the pound—once I had found it. The truck rolled in to Washington Square Park just in time to set up for a performance of *The Cherry Orchard*.

Don't let it happen to you.

Notes for the Producer

There will be many better producers of gorilla-theatre shows than I ever was. You can be one of them. That's an easy prediction to make, as I am such a poor producer. I was, at best, the first person to put together producing solutions for the emerging aesthetic. My work was always ad hoc. A good producer looks to solve problems and make plans well in advance of the need for them—at a stage in the process when my head is usually still sitting in a foggy cloud of artistic and conceptual issues.

So many procedures have been improved and refined as Gorilla Rep's work has progressed, but there is much room to do even better. The technical solutions to the problems that dynamic environmental gorilla work creates are so much a part of the work that I believe they emerge as an integral part of the production. They shape the audience's experiences exactly as much as if a new building were purpose-built for every new show. The new architectural organization to the existing elements is essentially behavioral and conceptual—this is true. But the details and signs created by lights and facilities, in addition to those that are ambient in the environment, are so important to the artistic statement as to be inseparable from it. They shape the audience's experience and work in concert with the other artistic elements.

Matt Freeman as King Ubu in Washington Square Park, New York City, 2001. Photo by Benjamin Heller.

With the right relationship to the site, things can be tucked away. I still remember when Mark Greenfield discovered the efficacy of storing props in the Call-A-Head portable toilets that he had set up on site for Gorilla Rep's *Henry IV*. It was a technique that I adopted often. Mark's work was a rare asset to the early gorilla work, as he was an experienced producer in his own right before becoming the hilarious actor that so many Gorilla Rep shows relied on. He could be watched and relied on for good solutions to producing problems.

Gorilla shows and parks go together well. We've had a great run of it with Gorilla Rep. If there is one thing that a gorilla-theatre producer needs to keep in mind that is specific to the role of producer, it might be to keep the rights of all personnel involved firmly in mind. From time to time, we have run into minor parks officials who have felt compelled to discourage us from working on gorilla-theatre shows. The best tactic they seem to have is to subtly treat us like we are petitioning for a privileged use of public property. We are not. As I mentioned in Chapter 2, our country's constitution guarantees the freedom of speech as well as the right to assemble peacefully. These are not privileges, and they are not rights that can be suspended at the whim of a parks official, no matter how well intentioned.

Permits for public-property use are a way of managing these rights so that everyone can enjoy them on public land. Full cooperation with permit procedures should ensure you every gorilla-theatre use you need these wonderful parks for. When going by the book doesn't work, you need to call the ACLU and stand up for your rights, or we will all lose them.

At the time *UBU IS KING!* was banned from Grand Central Terminal in New York City (described in detail in chapter 2), as an artist, I had to maintain my spirit and the spirits of the cast. As the producer of the show, I had to work hard to get it back on track, and I had to take every publicity opportunity that came along in the process. It was, in the end, a heck of a launch for the new company and aesthetic—and we were covered extensively in the *Village Voice*.

The procedures and habits that you develop and adopt for your specific locale will develop as you evolve your gorilla-theatre techniques. They need to be created to support what is going on, not to limit it. One thing that will help is learning to let new solutions be tried, even when you are not fully sure that they will work. "You may be right" is usually the best response to a new idea, even if it is not the one you end up using. Collaborating with your gorilla-theatre group does not mean giving up the ideal of making your work excellent—just the opposite. Someone needs to be relied on to choose the best practices, and that is part of the producer's job in gorilla theatre.

chapter **nine**

Documentation Practices

Documentarian

It may be possible to combine the projects of documenting and storing the documentation on your gorilla-theatre efforts into one job description, but we have found it difficult to do so. Original contributions from collaborating artists in film or video are one thing, and documentation is another—both interesting, worthy projects, but they need to be kept separate. The ephemeral nature of the theatre is something that will never be truly recordable except in the experience of the audience, in their hearts, minds, and souls. Even more so with gorilla theatre. Still, the effort to do so has yielded some interesting results.

That there was no uniform procedure for fully documenting Gorilla Rep's earliest production performances was in large part due to lack of funding. We never found a volunteer to organize these efforts, or a system to make them uniform, and so there is no record of many of the individual performances. In the early days of Gorilla Rep, video was of such low quality as to be laughable as a possible commodity if used to record live performances. The idea of selling these videos was silly. Still, the stage actors union was very strict about them, even for documentary purposes, and even in unpaid gorilla shows. As image quality improves, however, it makes more sense.

Photo Strategies

When a camera is present at a gorilla-theatre show, the best way to improve the result is to ask the actors to treat the camera as another audience member, just like all the others. This is interesting to watch in itself, and helps to prevent the camera from being an unnecessary distraction to the audience. As a simple but effective technique, it has also helped make representations of Gorilla Rep in the media interesting to look at.

The best photographs of the many good ones taken of Gorilla Rep productions are, to date, those taken by Benjamin Heller. His association with the company over a number of years grew out of his fascination with low-light photography and his enjoyment of Gorilla Rep shows. By watching a number of performances, Ben developed an eye for when Gorilla moments were about to happen and captured many of them on film. At a certain point, Ben even took some acting lessons with me, and I believe it had a good impact on his visual artwork. Happily, the media often called us for photographs, and Ben could provide them—gaining good exposure for our work and his. To cultivate this kind of rapport with another artist is a rare opportunity, and the more of them you can have, the better and more fulfilling your gorilla theatre will be.

In set-ups for publicity photos, I have found it best to take an edited piece of the play, perhaps a few gestures and words, and have the actors repeat them over and over with varying levels of intensity. When you ask experienced photo models to move their heads a bit to the right, they will move it perhaps a millimeter or, at most, two. This presents a completely different plane of their face to the camera and is sufficient. Actors, on the other hand, inexperienced with print work, will move their faces a few feet in response to the same request. It is good to warn your actors of this, and to ask them to respond accordingly for the camera operator and the art director if you are not art-directing the shoot yourself.

If you are art-directing, keep a few basic tips in mind. My experience has been that editors, online and in print, like two-shots. These are pictures of two actors, in character, in a dynamic exchange. If faced with limited resources, I would shoot this kind of shot only. Sometimes, they seem to like big, dynamic groups, but that is usually in the happy event that they cover a large part of the newspaper page with the picture. For a promotional shot, for your Web site or a color postcard, it is better to have fewer characters and to avoid bold, close-up shots. These aesthetic guidelines seem to produce images reflect the gorilla-theatre "feel" visually.

When you are done, take a look at the result and ask yourself with brutal and thorough honesty: Would I be interested in this if I were seeing it for the first time? Would it make me want to see the show? Develop your eye—it is the visual equivalent of writing good press-release copy.

Video Strategies

The video camera is a flexible thing, and I incorporated it as a character into an early Gorilla Rep production called *Sailing to Byzantium: Plays, Poetry, and Lyrics of W. B. Yeats.* It was an indoor gorilla-theatre show. The camera, as a character, represented History itself and the knowledge that all of the characters had that their deeds would be sung into the far reaches of time. C. Elliot Deal had begun work on the project as he created the video document of the paratheatric rehearsal process for *Sailing to Byzantium*, which began the rehearsal process at a beach in Lewes, Delaware. Ultimately, we had three video screens in the lobby of the space, one showing rehearsal footage, one showing this paratheatric document, and one showing a live feed of the audience entering the building to see the show. It was dynamic and interesting work, and I'll discuss it more below.

Other times, the video has followed the show like an audience member. Mr. Deal's experiments with this, again in the early days of Gorilla Rep, went over quite well on public-access television. Still, in those early days, our Gorilla Rep actors were not union members, and as success brought more union actors it certainly complicated things in terms of releasing video, even for nonprofit purposes.

The indoor gorilla-style play that I wrote but could not ultimately afford to produce was called *FrankInMind*. Here, again, the cameras were envisioned as an integral part of the performance process. Not unlike the cameras at a sports event or concert, the cameras were to be mounted on a series of bicyclelike carts with long, giraffelike necks that would have cameras at the end that would articulate all around. They were to look like large, benign animals, poking their noses into things as the story went along. The story was to be that of a modern-day or, I should say, futuristic retelling of the *Frankenstein* story of Mary Shelley. This time, so-called artificial intelligence was to be explored in an unusually depopulated vision of the future.

The obsession with the inclusion of the camera as an element in the action is there and bears writing about. Peter Brook and Charles Marowitz prophesied the creation of gorilla theatre, as I learned long after I had created it, so here is a note for a future iteration of performance: inclusion of even greater numbers of the audience through cameras as a part of the action in the dynamic gorilla environment.

The video camera is usually more flexible in its application to on-site documentation. As a rule, the best documents come from camera operators who have first taken in a few performances to orient themselves to the show and to map out basic paths from one scene-site to the next. After that, given enough well-charged batteries, the experience is relatively effective in communicating the general feel of a gorilla production. On the whole, the "hand-held" aspect of even the steadiest transition works well, and especially points out my long-standing contention that the audience on the move can hear every word of the scene that they are traveling toward while they are moving in such a transition. The keys to an accurate document are the cameraman's understanding of what he is seeing, and letting the actors treat the camera as an audience member.

Archiving: Print, Video, and Mailing Lists

There is nothing so frustrating as losing control of some aspect of your production apparatus. This is a risk, however, when you follow the much-lauded dictum of delegating the work to be done on the production side of things. In the case of documenting the work, delegation is often demanded by the simple volume of work that a gorilla-theatre production requires of the director. My experience has shown that getting a copy of all documentation is very important. I have little of it to show, because some people who have done it did not give me copies before disappearing!

If you cannot find a professional videographer, here are a few basic filmmaking tips that I have found helpful. Keep careful records, even short ones, about what is being shot. These are the equivalent of what filmmakers call "camera reports," and they will remind you of what you did later. Give the tape a serial number and a date on the case (there is nothing more frustrating than a pile of unmarked tapes when you need to find some footage). The camera reports note concisely the date, time, location, personnel, and what is being shot. You should make sure that someone other than you has a copy of the camera reports—stage management or your production manager. At least keep a backup copy, because these can become important years later.

It is often hard to explain why things need to be done a certain way to fit in with the work as a whole. But delegate and share the load you must—as an artist it is essential even though there are so many stories

Alex Roe as Macbeth at Fort Tryon Park, New York City, June 1999. Photo by Benjamin Heller.

about artists done wrong by putting their trust in others to get the work done. Documentation is imperative. There are some actors who will jump at the chance to see even the most poorly shot piece of video of a gorilla-theatre show if they have never been in one before. It seems to give them a useful context and lots of helpful clues about what exactly goes on in a gorilla-theatre show.

When something goes wrong, or is done wrong, or simply needs to be done again, having kept a record of what things were like earlier is extremely valuable. I know this is true for many things, but in the gorilla-theatre environment it seems that things are just a little bit more likely to go wrong. The simple example of a mailing list comes to mind. If you have kept an updated copy of your mailing list, you can use that one if the main copy is compromised, damaged, or stolen.

Everyone has a scrapbook. This is even more essential as you build a body of gorilla-theatre work. The responses to the work will vary and, over time, be useful as an adjunct to your efforts. I have often said that directing is a dialogue not only with audiences but with criticism as well. Keeping records of criticism builds up a very useful database of reaction to your work, and will be one of many factors that shape your ongoing research into gorilla theatre.

chapter **ten**
Design Issues and Aesthetic Practice

Lighting

A powerful way to directly cue your audience is certainly by use of your lighting. A semicircle of footlights will invariably let them know that it is all right to go right up to the instruments and form their front row for that scene. Even a ten-foot throw, directed down from three points around a circle, will form a pool that clearly says "here's where the action takes place in this scene." A single light, placed closer to the actor, will give a more closed-in and claustrophobic effect. As when Macbeth calls for his armor, this can be used to great advantage.

If you are less used to getting actively involved in the lighting, a certain amount of experimentation in the rehearsal room can give you a familiarity with the techniques. Of course, an able lighting designer never hurts, but it has been my experience that you will need them in the rehearsal room at an earlier stage than you are used to with indoor theatre. It might be worthwhile to have them see the work-through-level rehearsals with some of these lighting experiments under way.

Lighting Experiments

Flashlights and Angles—Moving Sources

This exercise is simple, and gives the actors in the scene the feeling of light surrounding them and reacting to their movements. Take at least two large, strong flashlights, and let actors carry them, crouched around a circle, in the darkened studio. The actors in a particular scene work in the circle, running the scene. As they do so, the actors crouched around the circle move the lights to keep the faces of the acting actors in the light's focus. This can enhance the mood of the scene in many ways, and the actors inside the circle should be encouraged to use this to their advantage. If possible, a third group of actors should be encouraged to observe these effects. Then, the three groups should shift to so that they each get to act, light, and observe—and again, so that the benefits of the lighting and observing can be tried in the acting.

Slide Machine and Area Lighting

Before using larger lights, a work-through can be created for a scene using only a slide projector. With only the white light showing, the actors can take turns moving the light so that it influences the scene being worked on. Later, it is possible to create different moods by adding slides and playing them over the action as well. Also, a variation with the slide projector staying in a fixed location often helps—this allows the acting to be shaped around the light, and uses the light to experiment with achieving the goals of the scene being worked on.

In a small theatre in Ireland, I was able to attempt an interesting experiment with light. Due to the nature of the repertory work that the company took on regularly, an extensive plot of lights was hung, focused, and circuited. In fact, much of the company's lighting stock remained hung in the grid even though it wasn't being used for a particular play. It was left there from seasonal special shows and shorter dance programs. It was all controlled by a then state-of-the-art board and, fortunately, a technician who knew his way around it, and the grid, very well. For a gestural pastiche that I was working on, we were able to ask the actors to simply work through the piece, trying to include whatever lighting was going on. Then, we created a number of different "feels" to lay over the work, pulling in the cues that worked. It was a brief workshop experience, but it left me feeling that the production we were working on could have handled a gorilla-theatre presentation. The gestural pastiche on the grid formation that we used on stage overlaid each gesture with a Gaelic word. Each character had at least three gestures to do, including one crafted for their name. It was an abstract opening to the piece, and the gestures were by no means literal or clichéd. In a way, I think it was also a dynamic way to introduce the audience to the fact that this troupe, essentially dancers, were about to act a powerful scene in a powerful way. The actors' own discovery that not everything needed to be locked into place, and that their generative participation as artists was essential to the work, showed as well, lending a special energy to the work.

Matthew Daniels as Valentine in *Faust* at Bryant Park, New York City, July 1997. Photo by Benjamin Heller.

Lights have represented fire, as in the "little touch of Harry in the night" scene in *Henry V* in gorilla-theatre shows. Puck has picked up lights and shone them at the audience. We've never used headlights, to be honest. They are too broad and unfocused. Also, they are pointed down, at the road, and don't end up doing much other than attracting attention to themselves. It's a good example of a cute idea that doesn't work. Too many artists think that cute ideas, by the mere virtue that they are cute, must work. The facile is not always the real, and lights are the best example of that. I often remind the actors that if the lights are shining in their face, they are well lit. As a professional lighting designer, I have conceded to an actor's complaint about lights shining in her eyes exactly once. Later, the director asked me why she delivered a particular monologue in the dark when the rest of the show was so well lit. I guess if he had caught me in the process, we could have corrected the problem. Her complaints had been strident and embarrassing around the other actors and crew, and I took stupid, petty revenge.

   Lights really are unforgiving. If you can't see an actor's face, it affects the drama extremely. Subtle control of the psychological effects and possibilities is to be left to real artists in the field, like Jason Boyd. If you don't have access to such a genius, an amateurish too-complicated light design can drag your show down inexorably.

Props

Anything mentioned in the text that directly affects the action needs to exist on stage, or it will risk becoming a sight gag. The fact that it is not there will seem funny. I can think of one instance where this effect was appropriate: in *Romeo and Juliet* when the servant, asked what is being carried, says, "things for the cook, sir, but I know not what." There are other props that seem unimportant, but are. All the brilliant acting in the world can't make it plausible that Imogen's servant in *Cymbeline* says, "I thrust this sword from me," without actually tossing away a sword. A small piece of Shakespearean stage business, perhaps, but it takes on weight when executed properly. That said, gorilla-theatre props need to be durable, referential, clear, washable, and storable—which usually means light or collapsible. Strangely, the more perishable a prop is, I have found, the less interesting it is on the gorilla-theatre stage. This may be related to the symbolic aspect of props in a story that is clearly told. The prop takes on more meaning to the audience than the characters know, and this need to be reflected in the design of the props.

An example of this would be the meats that Petruchio has brought in to Kate in *Taming of the Shrew* and then tosses around the room, complaining that they are overdone. I found a variety of dog toys at a pet store. The toys were shaped and painted to look like pork chops and other cuts of meat. They were just slightly—just the right amount—bright and toy-like, but also fairly realistic when seen from a distance on a "silver" tray. Those cheap plastic serving trays look nice and can take a beating as well. Now, at this point in the story, Kate is very hungry. Even as the audience realized that the "food" was, in fact, dog toys, it made them think that she was hungry enough to eat one. The association with dogs played up the element of dominance in the game that Petruchio was winning, and the toys looked great getting flung around the set. We ended up feeling like they were not very appetizing but that Kate just didn't care. Our Petruchio entered the scene humming the "Imperial Battle Theme" from *Star Wars II* just slightly off key, and the whole thing had the audience in stitches.

In *UBU IS KING!* I needed a set of swords that would look menacing and crazy at the same time. Ubu's mad tax collectors and the armies in the story needed to have some kind of weapon that would fit the design and also be abstract enough for the audience to project their own mad meanings onto them as well. It goes without saying that they needed to be phallic in a comic way as well. I decided on a design that was wacky and not very threatening, and I executed the design in thick plywood covered by a thin layer of papier-mâché. The effect was perfect, as these weird, free-form swords were carried with a dangerous-looking weight. They were heavy enough that the more delicate members of the cast needed two hands to wield them, and the cumbersome nature of the weight added to the comic effect. Yet beneath the ridiculousness, there was a threat—a piece of wood that size and weight really is dangerous!

Once, I commissioned playwright Kirk Bromley to totally rewrite *Beggar's Opera*, and I wrote some music for it. In Grand Central Terminal, the worst thing you could do would probably be to pull a real gun out, especially a .45 pistol. It would cause a panic. And, what is worse, it wouldn't be funny at all. Both would be problems for a production of *Beggar's Opera*, especially a novelty-jazz slapstick comedy version. And yet, one of the characters, hilarious in a gangster-style pinstripe suit and spats, has to pull a gun and wave it around. The character's name was Matty the Piece, so there was no getting around giving him his namesake weapon. I thought about using a toy weapon, but the scale was wrong and there would still be that moment of wondering what no one can help wondering in a big city—that's not a *real* gun, is it? A toy weapon has no weight. Also, most actors have never handled a real gun, and so unfortunately look really stupid on stage when they hold one. It gets waved around and dandled like a squirt gun or forgotten about entirely during dialogue. Believe me, when you hold a gun, the one thing you never, *ever* forget is that you are holding a gun. I wondered, what would make a gun even *more* dangerous than it already is? The answer hit me pretty quickly—a straight-up clown solution. Many clown props are made out of foam that is then coated with latex. What would make a gun more dangerous is if it constantly flopped around out of control like a length of hose, even though it could still go off to lethal effect. So I built an oversized foam gun. It was black and shaped like a .45, and it was so nose-heavy that any attempt to "aim" it made it sway from side to side comically. It was the actor's unerring comic sense that came up with the idea of stuffing it into his jacket, really jamming it in there so that when he drew it, there was a real cartoonlike expansion came up to full size . The barrel would unfold last, slowly becoming semistraight and refusing to

Christopher Carter Sanderson plays mandolin while Michael Colby Jones enters as Duke Orsino and says, "If music be the food of love, play on!" in *Twelfth Night* in Fort Tryon Park, New York City, 2000. Photo by Benjamin Heller.

point directly at what he wanted to aim at. Of course, he and the other actors worked up the reactions to this, ducking and cowering to get away from where it was pointing at any given second. It was a funny and durable gorilla-theatre prop, and helped tell the story well.

The ass's head in *A Midsummer Night's Dream*, part prop and part costume, is another example. For all of the critical and audience success of the production of *A Midsummer Night's Dream* in Washington Square Park, that head has been a constant source of thought for me. The piece I've used most often, originally built by artist Katherine Linton and restitched, reglued, and repainted many times over the years, is a big puppetlike mask with Bottom's face revealed through the neck. One year I used a hockey helmet with big ears sticking out of it, and that worked well too.

Sets

It often takes very little modification to make a big change in the way an area looks to the audience. You can use pruning shears, canopies, ropes, and rugs, and your design can accentuate the virtues of changing nothing physically, or the virtues of clever modification.

The local officials in charge of a park will want to know in advance about anything more or less permanent that you want to change. In general, it is best to think of making only temporary changes, unless a permanent change could also be seen as an improvement to the park. However, even permanent improvements in a park can be argued about, and trying them is most often an invitation into local politics, which is, in my experience, a game that the artist never wins. You will be lauded and applauded, even honored and encouraged, but actual change will never occur. The grants and help that local officials promise in order to get elected are routinely forgotten. The gorilla-theatre aesthetic is: get in, get the show done, and get out. Clean, simple, portable, temporary, and transient. Beauty itself, I would argue, is a passing thing. The ephemeral nature of gorilla theatre, even more than theatre with buildings and air-conditioning, allows for people to dream about it coming back to the park again. So, in the main, the way to change things in your gorilla-theatre environment is to always keep change temporary.

Ropes and twine can be used to hold back shrubs. An electrician can install a temporary electrical connection, or you can use a generator or vehicular power plant. When I mark an area or make signs showing how to get there, they are invariably with chalk on the sidewalk. This technique takes time and effort, and a certain amount of practice to make the print look good, but it is all worth it. Badly chalked signs look amateurish, and paper signs make it look like the cast is made up of temporary office workers. This may be the case, in fact, but the illusion that committed, trained, and talented artists are behind the whole thing is important to success. The idea that many temps are talented actors also is too much information for most people to hold in their head.

I've had good success with draping fabric over things in gorilla-theatre locations, but it takes a lot of cloth to have a good impact. A little here and there looks underdone, but enough can have the world-changing impact of a Cristo sculpture. The opposite seems true of flags. One or two here or there seem to do best—probably because of their symbolic nature. Draping a flag on the battlements of the war memorial at Fort Tryon Park gave new meaning to Macbeth's line "hang out our banners on the *outward* wall." We had a large parachute for our *Othello* set on Summit Rock in Central Park. It was huge and stretched over the back of the set, doing duty as Desdemona's bedspread. Other times, it lent a reminder of the centrality to the plot of a very intimate relationship. That is, it was a symbol of the bedroom. It was of adequate scale to be beautiful, taking on the shape of the rock and hill underneath it. It was pale cream colored and set off the darker rock and green grass very well. It could be held up to show shadow, and it had a great initial impact on the audience as they came upon the space, helping set the scene.

Usually I don't make any structural modifications to the scene-sites. However, when I have it has usually been to create levels. To be able to elevate a playing area in just the right part of the overall design can provide the audience with an even stronger cue to move, and it can increase the number of people who can effectively enjoy the experience of the gorilla-theatre show.

My brother made the most novel gorilla-theatre level for the actors that I know of. In the course of working on *A Midsummer Night's Dream* in Cumberland County in one of those first few years, we needed to get Puck elevated at various times for a certain sequence of scenes. My brother asked me how it should look; if we could put Puck anywhere, where would I have him appear during those moments? The answer was up a particular tree. However, it was a tree not easily climbed, and Puck needed to get up and down pretty quickly to make the action work in those scenes. I began to plot alternative solutions, but my brother calmly went to work. He lashed an aluminum ladder to the tree, which looked awkward and not very magical. Then, he put freshly cut branches of foliage in each of the tubes that formed the rungs of the ladder. The effect was subtle but of tremendous impact. The tree looked a bit ampler than most, but actually it looked better than it had. And Puck appeared to be able to run up and down the tree with ease.

Stage Fighting

The very best stage-fight choreographers, like James Hesla, have a knack for telling the story of the fight in such a way that scares and delights the audience without ever letting them think that the actors are actually in danger themselves. I believe that this best suits the gorilla-theatre aesthetic. Simulated fights with blood bags and so on are more for amusement parks and interfere with the progress of telling a good story. I suppose trappings like that might help spice up some stories, but that isn't what gorilla theatre is here to do. Weaponry is an important consideration. I have most often made concessions to the story and atmosphere in this regard than to any pretense of historical accuracy. For instance, in *Twelfth Night*, I used épées for the most part, giving the sheriff a heavy broadsword for effect. In *Macbeth*, it is broadswords all around, with the exception of axe, spear, and knife for the witches and murderers.

Frankly, broadswords look dangerous enough, and they're beautiful enough when handled well. They don't need blood bags. In his gorilla production of *As You Like It*, Andre Mistier had the character Oliver get beat up pretty badly. Here, a fun touch of "real" was just the style to choose for the fight. As it would happen, Dale Ho, the brilliant actor playing Oliver, also possessed a piece of removable dental bridge across one of his front teeth. In the course of the fight, he would spit out a couple of bright white pieces of candy after a staged blow to the mouth. Then, at a key moment, the fight would turn him around, he'd spit out the bridge into his hand, and turn back to the audience, supported by the two thugs. It was a truly hilarious effect. The effect of the tooth missing turned his handsome countenance into a fair imitation of Alfred E. Neuman. It was a very goofy look, and the juxtaposition really set off the humor. It was luck all around, but luck taken advantage of well by actor, director, and fight choreographer.

The good fight choreographers will teach, too. Actors who can really dance—Broadway dance—are usually the best at picking up gorilla-style fight choreography. It's possible for an actor to pick up bad habits in the wrong stage-fighting classes, but in the right hands, even an inexperienced actor will feel confident and execute the fight choreography well. We had one choreographer, Laurie K. Miller, choreograph a season of *Macbeth* with such grace that you would never have guessed that the actor playing Macduff had never touched a broadsword before his first rehearsal that year. The combat choreography was clear and carried the action forward in ways that allowed the actors to act while the fights were going on. This is the great risk, perhaps with all fight choreography: that the acting will stop for the fight choreography to happen. This is an accepted practice with more improvisational outdoor theatre, where the fight choreography really is much more interesting than the melodrama or banter that is passing for drama. Gorilla theatre is constantly dynamic and multilayered, and the communication is on many different levels simultaneously. "Cute" combat for its own sake just doesn't fit. A fight director like Laurie will build up these layers during the rehearsal process and facilitate the acting.

The fights need to cover distance within the scene-site. For one thing, this gives everyone in the surrounding audience a unique vantage point on different stages of the action. This action also needs something from the staging. As it must serve to tell the story most importantly, should have no further burden put on it. To be specific, I have not seen or conceived of a fight that moved the audience from one scene-site to another that was effective at telling its story. Monologues do it well—Jeffrey Kitrosser in *Henry V* is a good example. But fights somehow need to be fights and also accomplish their work with the focus of the audience stationary for the duration of the conflict. For one thing, in a good fight the focus of the audience is manipulated in a way that enhances the action. This is difficult enough in the round. Taking the audience along on a walk for a monologue that is specifically designed to be directed at them anyway can be a lot of fun, like walking along with a friend while they talk about something interesting. But moving with a fight induces distance and makes it hard to keep the audience away from swinging blades and flying bodies. Also, any dialogue during a fight can be lost with the audience struggling to establish their points of view. The moves of the fight are like important words that are spoken, and to hear them metaphorically we need to concentrate on them being spoken. The actors speak the fight clearly and well, but the audience needs the extra focus to understand it—most folks don't watch sword combat every day. They pick it up fast, though, and the still frame of their attention sets off the flashing fights well. Soon, they are moving to another space, and the fight is a hot memory, adding to the experiential and behavioral framework of the next scene.

chapter eleven

Indoor Environmental or Action Theatre

I believe that the subtlety that exists in a fully articulated gorilla-theatre production can be given added force indoors. Gorilla Rep has toured enough gorilla-theatre shows in interior locations to see that the switch is an easy one for the actors to make once they are aware of the issues at play and the direction of the indoor version. It is important to let them know where you feel the show is and where you think it can go given the new opportunities created by the indoor-performance form. Also, it is possible to generate indoor shows that move from place to place as they go from scene to scene in a truly gorilla fashion. I have had the best success with charging admission fees for indoor shows as the audience is on their on the way out, asking for a suggested donation. Most "suggested donations" are poor attempts at disguising the for-profit loss recoupment model of theatrical producing on a small scale. Not so at the Metropolitan Museum of Art, where you can give them a penny and get in, or pay whatever amount below the suggested donation that you can or wish to. This way of handling gorilla shows indoors has generated warm feelings and better cash flows than any Off-Off-Broadway theatrical production that I have seen or heard tell of.

The importance of indoor gorilla-theatre staging is that it provides a safe platform for some people to learn the style of viewing that a gorilla show benefits from. It takes some folks a while to watch what is going on and move in and out of participating in the scene shifts, even outdoors. Indoors, the space becomes informed by the motion in a different way. The audience, on stage because the whole space is the stage, become part of the set in a way that is even more focused, and can be even more dynamic, than outdoors. The scale of the indoor venue can be surprisingly huge and the effect is still the same. In an armory literally city blocks square in Scranton, Pennsylvania, *A Midsummer Night's Dream* became, appropriately, the first gorilla production to attempt the indoor shift. It worked, and it worked well. As each scene shifted, the audience left behind more of the folding chairs that they had insisted on deploying before the first scene. The shadows of the flashlights that we used intermittently to augment the larger lights we had up on poles cast shadows on the ceiling, and our ancient Athens took on a new kind of focus. Even the daytime show, when the sun poured in and changed the effect, was a success. In fact, the heightened focus was needed, as we had about five times as many students for that matinee than we had expected. What we thought was to be a show for about a hundred students turned into an entertainment for more like five hundred. They were an interesting set, but an attentive one, and we walked away with our commission intact and a lot of data on indoor gorilla theatre.

Design Issues

Remember that the indoor environment has a design to it. Treating it as a vacuum will backfire, but if you enhance it in just the right way, the results can be magic. As you will see in more detailed description in the section on examples, I incorporated organic, natural elements into the scenic design of *Sailing to Byzantium*. So far, my limited budgets have prevented me from putting all of the dynamic indoor environments in my mind into practical use in production. Still, selection is as creative an act as generation, and the bedroom scene in *Cymbeline* certainly drew enough compliments to be considered design. Indoors, it would have done very well to replicate the little "room" framed on three sides by shrubs. It read as a four-poster bed, and it seemed all the more a violation of intimacy when Cloten insisted on coming near. When Katherine Gooch as Imogen was asleep, she was prettier than Snow White. Indoors, there was the incredible swinging rope work of the Villa Villa ensemble, who created *De La Guarda*, to be pirated and used for dramatic purposes. I asked them if I could use it and they said that they wouldn't mind. Their work is more universal—so stylized and nonvocal as to be considered dance by many (including Actors' Equity). I look forward to directing *The Tempest* up in the air one day—I have the storm all planned out, and it will be good practice for the orbital, zero-G *A Midsummer Night's Dream*.

Indoors, the play of light and shadow actually needs more attention than it does outdoors. Outdoors, there is very rarely a total darkness. Some kind of ambient light is almost always present. Indoors, it is not possible to leave the audience in total darkness and expect them to make a good transition move—unless you give them flashlights. I did try the experiment of giving the audience strong flashlights once—but only once. I thought they'd light the action for themselves. I guess they weren't used to having this much impact on a production's action, and there were far too many wandering flashlights. Besides this, any flashlight strong enough is tiring for most people to hold.

In *Sailing to Byzantium*, the play of the shadows against the wall and the silhouettes of the actors served as an effective multiplier of the cast for ensemble chanting and movement.

The design of scene-sites in an indoor gorilla-theatre production is usually about shifting the orientation of the audience to the entire room, and lights are clearly a big part of manipulating the attention to various parts of it. A circular pool of light coming from one direction focuses eyes and feet and attentions. The redirection of attention makes slight-of-hand, overlapping scene shifts possible.

The ear is sharpened in a different way indoors as well, and effective silence is possible in a way that it never is outdoors. It is the equivalent of total darkness and creates a frame axis along whose coordinates things can happen. The awareness of this aural landscape in your design will help the actors adapt their message to the new, artistically controlled surroundings if you are moving indoors from a park or other outdoor location.

Indoors, also, the changing of costumes is a different matter from outdoors, and Theatre du Soleil is a good example of how this can work and how it can add to the drama. They usually provide a view of the actors preparing to go onstage.

Audience Changes and Pressures

I think that the audience's discomfort at the initial encounter with choice and interaction with the work is heightened indoors. It takes even more than the usual number of changes that enhance the experience to snap them into the behavioral mode of active participation, or "clearly acknowledged seeing," or "known hearing" or "subtle feedback recognition," or whatever it is that operates so clearly when it works. Knowing this can help you prepare for it and invite it with behavioral cues. Music has helped, when applied properly, and there are numerous ways for each audience member to get into the way of moving that is comfortable for them. It is clearer, perhaps, that some people are "getting it," and this helps bring the audience in. In my mind, it is like sitting by the fire in a big hall, telling stories. We just use more of the hall to play in, and new ways of playing.

Does a scene-site indoors promote an expectation of sitting or standing? Is this expectation played against or with? How does this affect the action? How does it relate to the story, moment by moment?

Applying outdoor environmental aesthetics to indoor staging . . . it sounds dangerous, doesn't it? It can be very powerful, and the key is maintaining the focus on the audience. This remains the same in both milieus, and all of the new resources that it brings behaviorally are the stuff of gorilla theatre, indoors and outdoors. The audience response to the essential aesthetic truths is different, but the sensitivity to them must stay the same. The way these responses charge the air provides a responsive frame, and you must articulate the staging in tremendous detail to make it work for you. When this detail is achieved, the experience is magical. "The key is that the work is never truly done," as one of the actors, Jy Murphy, would say. "Even the notes you give us encourage the growth. You'll sometimes ask us to just think about a moment, and not immediately demand how or even why." That paradox—that it is the same thing every night but totally different—translates just as well into a loft or large bare theatre as it does into a park. There is freedom for the audience and growth for the actor, and together they can dress the inside of a room with more fantastical colors than all of the lighting budgets on Broadway could. The activated imagination in behavioral fugue is collective here in a true sense. Each individual choice, each tiny moment, adds to the way the story is told in each performance. Yet, it is the same story and the recognizable gorilla-theatre groove.

Examples

Following are a few examples meant to tease out some design issues, questions, and problems that might help you as you work.

SAILING TO BYZANTIUM

Sailing to Byzantium had a design based on magical symbols and three long platforms set equidistant in the middle of the large loft on twenty-fifth Street in New York City.

As I mentioned in chapter 9, the video camera was the character of History, presenting a visual cue to the notion that the characters had knowledge that they would be storied in legend. The novel entrance of video art provided an atmosphere that seemed full of the sea and of heroes and tales from long ago, told, perhaps, at a contemporary beach barbeque. There was a line of chairs around the edge of the space, next to the wall, and a drum kit at the end of the space opposite the wall of magical symbols. The masks lived with the symbols on that wall.

There were plates of white paint and water on each platform. I had learned from some early experiments that the application of paint onto an actor's face on stage could have a magically transformative quality. And washing off the paint could be a part of the dramatic action as well. Especially because the costumes for *Sailing to Byzantium* picked up the trope of white costumes from *A Midsummer Night's Dream*, the white paint made a real design link between the actors' faces and the framing white costumes. This motif of flat white color applied over an organic surface was picked up on the corners of each platform, which had small trees attached to them; these, bereft of foliage, were painted flat white. Against the black walls and floor, the white trees went up to the ceiling, which was also white, making the threefold world of most metaphysical tales concrete in the space.

The three platforms individually, and the two spaces in between, counted as four distinct separate scene-sites, with the fifth consisting of all three used together throughout one scene. The sixth was the space that ringed the platforms, and the space between them and the walls. These modes seemed clear to the audience, judging by their behavior. The audience alternated very radically between the passive and the active, whereas the outdoor environment may allow for slow audiences now and again but never (to my experience) one that didn't move at all. Indoors, there were the same kinds of undeniable nodes of attraction— sight lines providing one. Also, seeing other audience members having a good time, getting close to the action, was a big invitation to the dance.

HAMLET

Hamlet was the thesis production for my work at New York University as an undergraduate. It was, as I have mentioned, the show for which I invented the paratheatric rehearsal process. In a large, Off-Broadway performance space, the production area was stripped down to its walls. There were graduated platforms on either side, the short sides of the rectangle, and taller, thinner ones along the long sides. The entire platform system was painted black, and the sparseness of the surrounding environmental-style set was compensated for with large amounts of lighting instruments and effects hung in the grid. The chapel was especially beautifully rendered as a soft coral-colored cross projected onto the wall. Likewise, the fire of the guards and the red dawning sun were depicted with washes and shapes of light. The sound design was enhanced by a set of sub-woofers placed at strategic angles around the space and hidden from the audience's direct line of vision. Sound designer Rick Nance recorded, mixed, and designed a series of fantastic sounds that made the world of the play incredibly deep and complete. We used a live voice-over of the actor playing Claudius for his brother the ghost's voice. The voice-over booth was visible up on a balcony, where there were also a few seats available for those unable to move around comfortably. They were able to watch the rest of the audience having a better time running around as the scenes shifted location down below.

It was no small feat pulling off an interesting production of *Hamlet* as undergraduates, but we all managed to do it. It was the pervasive sense of storytelling and dynamics that I think saved the show in the end. I followed the old dictum of staying mum about not having directed Shakespeare before, and fortunately no one guessed it was my first time.

It raised a question, one that comes back from time to time, about people sitting on hard floors. In parks, there is usually some soft grass to sit on, at least for some of the scenes. This is ideal. I have joked about selling gorilla-theatre cushions, but I think I'll leave that to others. Over the years, audience members have gotten used to thinking this issue through for themselves.

THE CELIBATE

The Celibate was produced in the basement of an Eastern Orthodox church near Second Avenue in the East Village. That makes the environ-

Left to right: Christopher Carter Sanderson, Amo Gulinello, and Jy Murphy in *Talking Jazz* at the Duplex, New York City, April 1997. Photo by Benjamin Heller.

ment sound small, and I used this assumption to good effect. There was a front room that presented itself as a conventional church basement, although it was large enough to handle an audience of fifty or so and still leave us room on the stage area for the action. The story we were telling was of a group of people who had been changed by a catastrophic disaster; it had literally changed their minds and they each spoke their own fictitious language. At the end of the first half of the play, another disaster destroys the hotel they were all living in, and they go on a journey, both an internal and an external one. It is a journey through many "lands," and we follow the two main characters. For comic relief, there are a pair of tourists who wander into the situation from "our" world.

For the second half, we invited the audience into the interior room, one un-guessed-at. It was really big. Imagine an old basketball court with very high ceilings. Although there were thin columns that would have presented an obstacle to sight lines for conventional theatrical settings, we left that area empty and had the action circle around it. The audience walked in with a lot of things already going on. In general, they hurried into the center and moved around it as the action circled around them. We could set up each "land" behind them while the current action was in front of them, and they could turn around and watch that, too, if they wanted to. The ensemble of characters for the first act had fantastic and colorful costumes to match their fantastical characters. In her role, Christina Cabot wore a big, shiny blue prom gown with a gorgeous décolletage and a pair of heels as she was revolving and playing charades in an alien language. Jack Haley and Ken Schatz were running around as a cook and a hen doing the classic "I'm going to put you in the pot" shtick. Kurt Ehrmann was dressed in a long, grand bellman's coat done all in dark brown and tan. This gives you an approximation of the luster of the first half. Kurt's character's name was "Winning," so, in a moment of trying vainly to explain himself in the midst of this delicious chaos, he could exclaim "I'm Winning!" and look even more baffled.

The sumptuous costumes of the first half were replaced with plain white sweats for the second half, and we used physical mass and kinetic body sculpture to create the lands that the characters journeyed through as the action revolved around and around.

Talking Jazz

Talking Jazz is a fun technique that I made up to perform at fund-raisers for Gorilla Rep and other companies when we were invited to help. It is a jazz bass and drum kit, sometimes augmented with other instruments, backing up an actor, who is performing a poem interactively with the music. Others do similar stuff, but this is my brand of "spoken word," and it has a particular flavor all its own. For one thing, I compose all of the music that backs up the actors, and I direct them in such a way that it all ties together. I'll keep a trade secret or two about it to myself. This cool jazz phenomenon has had crossover into gorilla theatre on a few occasions.

The actors stand up in the audience area to do our usual closer, "Footnote to Howl," by Allen Ginsberg. As the piece builds, it swoops around the crowd, and sometimes onto the stage, including everyone in the ecstatic metaphysical dialogue (or tri-alogue, depending on the night) of the piece. Although the audience hasn't gotten up to move around with the actors yet, I believe they would be welcome to; the true gorilla spirit visits the places where we perform.

chapter twelve

Moving a Show

Feel of the Show

Touring and staging for booked locations is a set of skills to learn, for both myself and the actors involved. As I look back on Gorilla Rep's production history to date, I believe that taking a show from an indoor location to an outdoor location is harder than the reverse. The long leap that makes a gorilla-theatre show different from merely being an indoor production strewn across a landscape is a hard one for actors to make. I acknowledge this. I have, happily, seen actors take it on as a challenge and regard it as a skill to be learned. This application has been invariably fruitful; two Gorilla Rep actors, Sean Seibert and Richard Scudney, positively bloomed in the gorilla environment. And these two men are very different actors, with different experiences, and a good ten years apart in age. Sean had a lot of barnstorming Shakespeare experience in the Midwest under his belt, and Richard came at it from a more traditional theatre background and college experience. They both stepped up to the challenge of working in a gorilla-theatre show, took it seriously and applied themselves, and turned in well-loved performances. And this in their first outings as gorillas. Sean blew apart the role of Bottom, and audiences loved it. Richard turned the fortune-teller in *Cymbeline* into a major focus of audience attention. Both were well-polished gorilla performances, with specific nuances built into the work for the demands of the medium. They prove my point, as countless other brilliant actors have done, that learning to use a gorilla-theatre performance to learn and use modifications in acting style is important. I believe that this is easier to do when going straight to the true outdoor gorilla-theatre medium.

Putting on a show indoors first risks ossifying old habits that will have to be unlearned before new ones are learned.

The Gorilla Rep production of *As You Like It* is an example of this. After rehearsing it for a gorilla-theatre production in Fort Tryon Park, I opened it at an indoor location. We had some high school charges over from the NYU summer enrichment program, and we allowed members of the club to see the show too, all for free. The result was a big, happy audience who laughed and had a great time despite their large disparity in ages. However, as successful as the Fort Tryon production then was, with big audiences, and happy ones at that, there was a lingering feeling of unrest in the cast when we moved back to the park. One of the actors arrived each day, roller-bag in tow, with an absolutely insupportable attitude, found a few crew members to bitch at, and then began the work of getting herself into the correct mental attitude to perform. It was as if that first night indoors had made her feel like she was now being demoted to the park, and she was constantly looking for the dressing room and other indoor amenities that the theatre had provided. I don't fault her for her rotten attitude. It was my fault for taking the show indoors with a cast of inexperienced gorillas. As correct as my intentions were, I should have known to launch the ship onto the waters that it was designed for first. It had been luck in finding more rugged actors that had kept me from seeing it before.

Moving A Midsummer Night's Dream: "Get Puck!" and Other Stories

GET PUCK!

We took *A Midsummer Night's Dream* to Camp Shohola in upstate New York once. It is a summer camp for boys, and the girls' camp came over to visit for the performance. We had a good, clear day of restaging and rearranging the scene-sites around the camp's soccer field. There were angles off the field on the embankment in one direction, and we improvised a few platforms out in the field, too.

The actors had the changes down, and we went smoothly through the cue-to-cue. Dinner went by, and we saw clouds begin to gather as we started the show. About halfway through the performance, it started raining too hard for the show to be effective in the soccer field. Now, we could have cancelled, or, given the dogged pursuit that the campers were engaged in, we could have just gone on. But I felt it better to take the per-

Ken Schatz and Christopher Carter Sanderson shine flashlights as campers watch Puck (Amo Gulinello) flying at Camp Shohola. Photo by Lynda Kennedy.

formance under the large awning that covered the nearby basketball courts. That transition was fast, and it went well. As I remember, the lovers just ran over there instead of to the planned platform, and on we went. These were kids used to sitting around campfires, so it was going well. The actress playing Hermia was more than equipped to keep a bunch of boys completely interested in the goings-on. Yet it lacked the dynamism of the scene-shifts. As the show went on, I kept my eye out for a chance to move back out under the stars with our powerful flashlights.

My opportunity came as Puck had a scene-shift coming up. The actor playing Puck, Amo Gulinello, and I quickly conferred off to the side, and he set up for the shift back out to the field. As he began to head back out, the actors lighting him rushed to support the move, as was best in the situation, and indeed in all hand-held lighting solutions. Perhaps I underestimated how anxious the campers were to get back to the gorilla-style staging. Or, perhaps the adrenaline level of our audience went up as the girl campers went back to their side of the lake to get out of the rain. Maybe it was enthusiasm for Amo's performance—he is an alumnus of the camp, after all. Whatever it was, it was triggered by one little boy yelling, "Get Puck!" The whole audience stampeded after Amo, who was running back to the field, and an unscheduled pile-up ensued. Just as there's an Australian Rules Football, this was "American Rules Shakespeare"!

By the time I reached Amo, he was buried under a pile of boys. I tossed them off, left and right, and dug him out pretty quickly, but I need not have been worried. He was all right and waved off the cut to jump right back into the action—as soon as I had liberated him from the pile, that is. What threatened to be another pile-up was averted as he took to one of the platforms and the lights caught up to him. The spell, unbroken, went on to cover the rest of the story.

Like the new attitudes of the lovers after they awake from the spell, there was a cool freshness to the air after that summer shower. The departure of the girls made the audience smaller, but more dedicated, and the play-within-the-play felt like a talent show and made the campers laugh just as much. Puck, who is the character who sees the audience most closely, was played by the actor who was the connection that brought the show to the camp. How had we been ready for the things that night would throw at us? We were ready to take risks. There is no art without risk, as many have often said. The risks are great in gorilla theatre, and the audience and cast share them as in no other theatre in the world.

Moving *Midsummer*

There are many stories about moving *A Midsummer Night's Dream* from its home in Washington Square Park: *Midsummer* on a courthouse lawn in Cumberland, Virginia; in the armory in Scranton, Pennsylvania, in an Off-Broadway theatre on Seventy-second Street in New York City; and so on. The common theme of adapting to these spaces has been our continuing concern for the audience's experience. The musical score of surprise and reassurance, of loud and soft, and the fugue of the plot interweaving with the inclusion of the audience as the rest of the cast, are merely rescored for the new instrument, so to speak. The detail that fills a gorilla-theatre show outdoors can be exposed in new ways indoors, if that's the demand, and the physical space that you are moving to should be considered by the actors vocally. A short series of experiments with the members of the cast watching snippets of scenes and then trading off usually takes care of this. As the actors see their colleagues using the space and its possibilities, they usually develop an idea for their own work pretty quickly.

As you place the scene in a new situation, the staging should be moved by the actors to compensate. A run-through if you can get it, or a cue-to-cue if that's all there's time for, should point up the places where you need to step in and help shape the new staging. It is better to give the cast a crack at it before you make major changes—they will more readily accept your modifications if they have already demonstrated to themselves how the new space handles.

Perhaps it is obvious, but a gorilla-theatre show always moves in quickly and well to the space it was originally designed for. This is actually a part of the beauty of tacking on a performance out of town at a paratheatric rehearsal location. It goes well, the audience loves it, and the actors are happy and all that more excited about bringing it to its intended location. "Arouse a sincere desire," as Dale Carnegie says.

At indoor theatres, *A Midsummer Night's Dream* has always sought out new ways to use the space, even with the audience stationary in comfortable seats. Audience entryways have become hills for the fairies to climb over, and the obligatory aisle scenes have occurred. When possible, we've gotten the lovers, with Theseus and Hippolyta, into the audience to watch the play-within-a-play.

When it has moved to outdoor locations, I have always been pleased to find people everywhere with the same set of internal navigators, the same enthusiasm for the discovery of the new form, and the same openness in providing insights and ideas about it. Once the actors experience the efficacy of the artistic selection of scene-site to optimize audience flow and traction for their attention, they will jump into a location change with enthusiasm. This has always been the case with our *Midsummer*. Other shows, too, but this one first. The invention of the aesthetic is tied up with this play. *Hamlet* was a precursor, but with *A Midsummer Night's Dream* in Washington Square Park the tools and the aesthetic became fully formed. After all, when it comes to paratheatric rehearsal, "there we shall meet for if we meet in the town we shall be dogged with company and our devices known." Every paratheatric rehearsal takes your players a mile without the town, metaphorically, to meet the fairies and to come back changed for performance after performance.

A gorilla-theatre show's music may be modulated indoors, but it is the same symphony that you have written in the park.

In a very real way, you can direct a show only once. I have often wanted to put three or four casts in repertory on the same play to show how differently a show can be directed by the same director and, if it worked, all to good effect. How much fun would it be to have one of the shows panned by the critics, and one well loved? Hard to imagine them all enjoyed by everyone, but I maintain it would be possible. Perhaps one directs the same play differently every time by definition. You have grown, one would hope, and brought depth to your interpretation. You work with different actors, and even when they are the same for a tour, different nuances can be played up. You'll have to leave such definitions up to those who define you, I suppose. Gorilla theatre hasn't been around long enough to be dismissed by those whom it threatens or fossilized by those who would trap it, and every gorilla production has new things to teach me and its audience. This is true of, and should be looked for in, each new location to which you bring a gorilla production.

chapter thirteen

Notes and Observations

Dialogue with Criticism

Critics pay a lot of attention to the theatre. They therefore watch forces moving through and around it with a special difference. It is a difference that can be frustrating, and it is a difference that can be the most instructive single force for a director, second only to the multiplied force of the audience itself. At best, the critic looks at how and why a production works—and it may be working on levels that you are unaware of. When it is not working, they will talk about why. As a director, this should make you cringe—until you think it through. Remember the magic words "They may be right," and take another look. You may find that you learn a lot this way. After all, they may be wrongheaded sometimes—human beings invariably are—but all the complaining in the world about a critic's power seems to accomplish only one thing: to make you look like a bad loser. It is interesting that when they make a call against a show, it is sometimes because they were not aware that the show was beginning a trend that would later render their ideas conservative in the extreme. I have seen a critic pan a show that had a houseful of people absolutely doubled over with laughter and buying CDs of the music on their way out. He saw traditions being broken, but he couldn't see that new ones were being made. Who can blame him? We live to direct another day, and we have not been killed, and our birthdays have not been taken away. One critic told me point-blank that I directed too many plays in one season and that if I wanted better criticism I'd better do less. How or why one would argue with advice like this, I do not know. You listen, and you either realize you are lucky to get it, or you don't. Remember, no one is more aware that they live in a world full of people than critics are, and if hundreds of people are cheering on your work every night, it is clear that criticism is a part of what's going on, but it's not everything that's going on.

Opening night at a gorilla-theatre show presents similarities to audition and paratheatric rehearsal. Having a writer or theatre critic along to observe rehearsals has been uniformly fruitful. The critics are there at opening night, too. Francine Russo's words taught me a lot about what was going on at a paratheatric rehearsal, and I have reread her *Village Voice* article when designing new ones and attempting to hone the technique. Elliot Deal was Gorilla Rep's resident film-creator for a time, and camera work recording the paratheatric rehearsal runs that he came along for served a similar purpose. There is a benefit from seeing the work put into a clear conceptual frame by a bright mind and able artist.

Actors face rejection again and again at your hand—do you mean any ill will toward the actors you do not cast? I think not. I hope not! They may come back and prove to be perfect on another occasion, for one thing. Especially in the gorilla theatre, they may go about learning what it is that the aesthetic demands and come back to surprise you. So, if you do not want the rejected actor to go away angry, you must think of criticism as an essential part of your education. When the whole world of the play works, the mise-en-scène itself extends to the writing about the show. This is often the anatomy of a hit. Those words that take some of the flame and color of the show and ignite the desire for fireworks in the reader's mind are important. James Ireland Baker went out of his way to write in *Time Out New York* magazine about a Gorilla Rep show that he loved and everyone who told me that they came as a result of that article has been happy about it. No one is omnipotent; if you were, you'd just force a good review of a bad play. You are too close to the work to judge and dissect it—in the gorilla theatre, your love of what you are doing and what you have made leads the audience into the work. When it works, they see at the very least something and at best something more than you saw in the work when you helped it all come together. Sure, some critics are tough, but who would have them any other way? Let's benefit from good criticism and be thankful for it. Gorilla theatre needs it in order to thrive and grow into the jungles of public spaces everywhere.

If the critic, on a very basic level, wants to be a part of the show as much as the rest of the audience does, and if you are including the audience in the show as an aesthetic principle, then your stance toward criticism should be a confident one. Good or bad, the criticism is a factor among other factors, and the work moves on. I have done many Gorilla

Rep shows where no critics showed up at all, and people still came in droves, had a great time, poured forth compliments, and sent their friends to see it. But I do know how important critics are. The director's dialogue with criticism is like the fisherman's dialogue with the sea. Critics are a force to be reckoned with. Gorilla theatre sets its sails in a particular manner. See to it that you do.

Relationship to Academia

And nothing can rob Shakespeare of his life in the theatre, or of his poetry, faster than an academic sensibility; it should probably be made a crime to teach him at all, except as part of an actor-training course.

—Michael Feingold, "No Great Shakes," *Village Voice*, July 30, 2002

A few teachers of college theatre know what they are doing. It is lucky and rare, of course, to find one of them, because they are few and far between. More often, even the best teachers will have ossified into a theoretical standpoint that prevents them from being in or directing shows for fear that their theories will thereby be refuted! And these are nice, concerned, intelligent, experienced people that I am talking about. Before I let loose more of this gripe about academe, let me give you the magic key. Find a teacher who is actively working on a show at least twice a year, and preferably twice a semester, and you probably have a real theatre teacher. Academic institutions tend to discourage theatre that engages the society at large, but it is essential that the theatre strives to live in every environment.

For one thing, in the Ivy League, held up by many as the acme of educational excellence in this country, theatre practice is a virtually ignored discipline. Moreover, nobody seems to have noticed that college professors are not required to have any credentials in what they are actually doing—teaching. The archaic notion that simply doing something well somehow magically makes one able to teach it prevails. More so with theatre, where one doesn't even seem to need to be able to do it at all to be presumed able to teach it. A director is only as good as his or her last show. The same goes for a directory teacher.

In this atmosphere, then, gorilla theatre is bound to make enemies, by its populist and popular nature. At Brown University, for instance, the gorilla-theatre group called Shakespeare on the Green receives nothing in formal support from the theatre program, as of this writing. Several of the group's student directors have studied with me and have assisted on Gorilla Rep shows before directing Gorilla Rep shows of their own in New York City, to great acclaim, and still the group receives nothing from the theatre program.

Princeton University granted requests to assist and in some cases even act multiple roles in Gorilla Rep shows at the outset, and then revoked their offers when the university learned that the work was to be gorilla theatre. The institution's deep bias against the arts, in particular the theatre, and against an established experimental style like gorilla theatre, was exposed. The students who could afford to do the work on their own did so, but others who could not afford to take advantage of the opportunity were left out. This after the university itself had hired me as a guest lecturer for a semester.

Yale University, on the other hand, has yielded a number of gorilla-theatre practitioners, and my years of teaching there in the undergraduate program resulted in several projects that moved to New York.

Success and the attention it brings are at odds with certain unwritten rules that exist in academic circles. For one thing, the illusion that the students are all buying a completely equal education is exploded by brilliant artistic work; those who are left behind and complain invariably poison the forces of academia to support further efforts. They also try to purchase success with everything at their disposal except hard work and dedication to the art form.

If young actors are straight out of college, forgive them. They are used to hour-long warm-ups, when you are fighting for space or paying for it. They have been at the top of their class and the envy of their school for playing large parts. The supporting roles you give them are a fantastic learning experience, it is true—and they will learn by being exposed to the unflappable professionalism and humility of the leads. People who have consecrated their lives to the theatre and have been rewarded are invariably humble. It is a humbling experience to have your work loved by audiences and to become known for good work. You know you are all too human and don't deserve the idolatry that can attend fame. After all, it is a false god and it harms those who worship it. The attention of the audience is the greatest payment, and their participation in the aesthetic makes the show better every night. They have shared the risk with you. Be appreciative. When I have been, I've been happy. When I haven't been, I've been miserable. Gorilla theatre changes things, and this, in turn, provides linkage to cultural forces that other theatres only dream of engaging. A university is a very pressurized society, oddly compressed. The waves break differently there, so be aware.

Much of the academic bias against practical artistic brilliance in general, the theatre in particular, and gorilla theatre as an extension is based on the much-trumpeted ideal that practical skills shall not be taught as a part of a liberal arts curriculum. Of course, you'll wander over to the chemistry department and see real experiments going on with real chemicals that yield real results, and they have practical industrial applications on a larger scale. The physics department at Princeton is being paid by the government to build real rocket engines and test-fire them in the basement! Learning advanced chemistry and then not going on to a career in it will leave one wondering about the use of studying it at all, whereas studying theatre and really making good theatre is related to presenting oneself, and this is of value in any profession.

Remember the 30 percent rule: only 30 percent of college graduates actually pursue the field of their major in school. Professionals often complain of their fear of public speaking and presentation. A gorilla-theatre show executed for real audiences provides real experience with public presentation to an audience that is far from the artificial listeners in speaking classes—it gives one experience in talking to people of all backgrounds. The arguments against theatre training are so vigorously defended and so patently false that the biases of the academia show all the more clearly.

Perhaps not coincidentally, the more professional and artistic the theatre department is, the more likely it is to actively send interns to work on gorilla theatre. A gorilla internship is harder than most theatre internships, but it is also a chance for student actors to get in front of large, expectant crowds and develop their talent immediately.

Academia, then, and the security of any academic position, is to be regarded by the gorilla-theatre practitioner as the Siren singing on a shore wracked with danger. Have yourself lashed to the mast! Do this by continuing to practice and generate work, building up a host of accolades and recognition as a master of the new form.

That said, Mr. Feingold's observations at the beginning of this section are relevant for more than just Shakespeare, and more than just gorilla theatre. But we need to keep this idea in mind: the academic approach to theatre seems to be, at its core, the fallacious notion that one can teach the audience that a miscast actor should be accepted in the role that they are mangling for some extra-artistic reason. There is nothing in most plays to dictate casting except the text and the need to articulate it well.

Sibling Institutions

There's no reason not to market and advertise your show in partnership with other shows and theatrical organizations. I've never had anyone complain about getting a few postcards for other shows in my programs. In the theatre, we don't compete the same way that other businesses do. Everyone should be going to the theatre every night and seeing everything there is to see. See a gorilla-theatre show tonight, see a Broadway show tomorrow night, and compare the two! This has always been my attitude, and it has worked well for my gorilla-theatre shows. Folks who see a lot of theatre love gorilla-theatre productions as much as everyone else does. Sibling institutions are sisters and brothers who can help you out, and you can help them, too. After all, if your gorilla-theatre productions are like mine in the first years, you'll work with actors on the scene who will come from and go to work with other companies. Let them carry the tale of good work and an open attitude. Let the audience judge them and you, and also see a lot of other shows.

There's no reason to make a new theatre company. There's no reason to make a new gorilla-theatre company, and there's every reason to make a new gorilla-theatre company. If you are building these shows, you need whatever support you can get. That others have done the same thing in New York City and elsewhere is no reason not to get started on your company. Nearly every small town in the country has a Shakespeare festival, and most have an alternative theatre space in some black box or over some bar. Bust out a gorilla-theatre company and some good gorilla shows, and let everyone else do it, too. The local Shakespeare company might compete, and that will educate audiences on the work—either by providing a staid, stale copy, or by giving you some competition of quality. Believe me, I have imitators, and it is much more sweet to me for them to be good and worthy than bad. Bad work is associated with the originator of the style too. When you bring gorilla theatre to your environment, there will be waves of reaction, and the good and the bad and the talk and the support and the competition, and I wish the storm of it on you! Joy of it. It is the storm that proves the soundness of the ship. It is not under ideal circumstances that a team is proven good.

The other side of the marketing coin is about aggressively looking to promote your shows at other people's expense. I don't recommend it. Better to look outside of the existing theatre promotions to find the gorilla-theatre audiences waiting to come to your shows. Creative and good casting and every element of quality will do most of the marketing for you. I have gotten more out of good work and free listings than any ads that I bought. People expect ads when they are going to pay for tickets. Taking out ads for free shows wouldn't work except perhaps with specific sponsors, and these have been hard to come by for me. You should look into this with more care, consult experts, and make it work better for your gorilla-theatre shows.

Long ago, when Ludlow Street was the axis mundi of Off-Off-Broadway in New York, companies in New York City would band together to present festivals of different works by the same author treated by different companies. Adaptations, and various interpretations, sometimes even of the same play, would run for weeks. This kind of collective tack might work well with a consortium of gorilla-theatre productions and companies.

chapter **fourteen**

Spirituality

To me, it is self-evident that a spiritual life is a basic necessity for survival as an artist. Religion is for people who are afraid of Hell, I was once told, and spirituality is for people who have already been there. "There and back," as another friend reminds me.

You know, if you didn't need this chat here at the end of the book, you probably would have skipped it. Instead you are reading it. Thanks for that.

There is a clear ethical imperative in gorilla theatre, and any ethics leads to metaphysics in the end, or in this case spirituality. I'm not here to argue semantics—call it pataphysics if you want to.

Gorilla theatre is a very sophisticated collective use of public places. This country associates collectivization for any purpose other than profit with negative things. The United States in 2002 witnessed many scandals over corporate ethics. And not once has anyone stated the clearest possible solution to corporate regulation: socialize business entirely. This would make every corporation transparent because it would make every citizen a stockholder in every business.

Not that anyone's going to listen to that in this country of capitalist puritanism. They will listen intently, though, to a good play that their children are enjoying. "Thanks to you, we have a six-year-old who begs me to take him to see Shakespeare in the park every night."

Making theatre in parks and public places because you think it is a cheap alternative to renting space is a fatuous and morally bankrupt idiocy. It is a mistake for which your audience will reward you with nothing but well-earned scorn. This is not mere speculation; I've seen that attitude eat poor hapless fools alive.

Once, as I stood watching a Gorilla Rep show, *The Taming of the Shrew* as I remember, a bright young actor turned to me in a musing frame of mind. "There are more beautiful women here in this audience per square foot than anywhere else I have ever seen. Why?" I did not hesitate, in what I meant to be a total joke: "Because our hearts are pure and our cause is just." Nuts, of course. Still, he and I sort of drew a breath. There is an ideal there, a value that I really do aspire to, even if I could never attain it.

> I'll never forget the joy of looking at my kids in the audience . . . among all those New York faces, from every walk of life . . . some of our Russian neighbors, Dominican kids who happened by and stayed, old, young . . . gathered together to watch . . . with the sun going down over the river . . .

A letter like this one puts it all in perspective. The actors are not the audience, and we all work for the audience together. When the actors become their own audience through months and months of needless rehearsal, they forget the importance of the audience and risk making only "drama" that has nothing to do with good theatre. All of the theory in the world cannot shield you from the truth. The audience is the reason that gorilla theatre is made, and the bad side of that might be egotistical attention seeking. So be it. The good side of it is a joy and an altruism unique to this work. Work and reward become one.

Good theatre is for all people. Even if that is impossible to realize in a given gorilla-theatre production, it is the right direction to follow. Can everyone enjoy your show? Populate your imaginary audience . . . its capacity is infinite, isn't it?

The following may come in handy. It has been called by Kurt Vonnegut the greatest literary contribution of the American culture to date: "God, grant me the serenity to accept the things I cannot change, the courage to change the things I can, and the wisdom to know the difference." You will be amazed at the game this plays with gorilla theatre, the part of the game that is gorilla theatre. I think James Carse called it the "infinite game," I think of it as "Calvin Ball" from the comic-strip *Calvin and Hobbes*, and Andre-Philippe Mistier wrote a song about it. All songs are about it. And there is a storehouse of wisdom called stories, and the telling of them may be the wisest part that they talk about. Gorilla theatre tells these stories, if you do it right, with a new link to what we all share in common. The more you think about what we all have in common, the more you are thinking spiritually. The most absolutely true spiritual practice may be that which does not demand membership in its organization to attain spiritual practice. Your religion is important to you, and it should be. Spirituality is something shared by all, no matter what religion says. Some people who are very shy about it will be introduced to it at a gorilla-theatre show. However, at a gorilla-theatre show, the openness to this possibility is to be a conscious part of the mise-en-scène.

All prophecy is self-fulfilling. Prophecy itself acts as a catalyst for attempts to fulfill it. This functions in the roots of a play when a character is predicting the future. Predicting the future is always an attempt to influence it, as anyone who plays the stock market knows.

People can mess with you, and "cut" procedure is your friend. There are bullies everywhere. It is a blessing to work without them arriving on the scene, and the big, happy audience will often help repel them anyway. People will enact their neuroses on you, and I have tried to make this a book about gorilla theatre and not theatre in general. There are better books for that. When in doubt, remember that no one can make you do anything that you don't want to do, and patience is a force more powerful than any. Keep your Krazy Glue in your pocket and your attention unwaveringly on the work.

Craftsmanship is key. Work over everything, think it out, and put your thought into action. Gorilla theatre will demand so much from you—so much detail. Every moment must be rich to the maximum of your capacity. So much that is prearranged in the theatre is unhinged in the gorilla theatre. So many constants become variables. Still, the attention to detail will yield results, and an ongoing understanding that you can trust will result. Mastery of the multivalent environment will bring you focus and depth, should you work in other aesthetics. I believe it is good service and right practice.

Remember to ask for help, in case you forget. Sometimes people are there for you, only waiting to be asked. Things change, favorable conditions will come, unfavorable ones will be handled. So many forces swirl around the gorilla theatre. How could we keep track of them all?

Theory and rhetoric be damned. Make a good show.

Build rest into the work whenever possible. There are a lot of things other than the work, of course. Someone once warned me that my struggle would be to keep the theatre a part of my life instead of subverting my life to the theatre, and he was dead right. Ironically, like rests in the work, keeping the work a part of my life has been best for the work, too. Maybe I mean "counterintuitively" instead of "ironically."

Keep the difference between colleagues and friends paramount in your mind as your success mounts. Not only in academia do the freaks dwell who would misconstrue you and twist your words. Rely on being honest, keeping your intentions good. Apologize when you know you've made a mistake, and people will be more tolerant of your experimentation. But keep from making the mistake of treating a colleague like a friend, no matter how solicitous they are. There is a difference, and thank God somebody pointed it out to me. It is a struggle to make the line clear, but it is so very much the right thing to do.

Stephen Wangh, ETW's master teacher and author of *An Acrobat of the Heart*, has a definition of experimental theatre that is good and sound. All theatre is experimental, and we collect reams of data at every juncture in the gorilla process, every moment in the show, every good, happy time, and every bad, sad time.

Everyone has his or her own way to go. Let them leave the gorilla show if they need to. They may come back when they are ready. The pressures on the actors may make it hard for them to stay too. Be as consistent as you can in the execution of your ideas, and keep your ideals and values clear. You'll have problems, you'll make mistakes. For such a sensitive art form and aesthetic idea, gorilla theatre is amazingly robust. Your colleagues will have muscle and thought to put into the work, and that is the essential fabric of the work. Maybe people will be disappointed in you, and it will hurt. Let it hurt and do not run away. The pain is a teacher.

ABC: always be casting. Why not? Even Copernicus himself (the performance artist, not the ancient astronomer) didn't think he could pull off King Lear. But pull it off he did. I dedicated myself to helping him, and he worked like an ox. The result was a ball to watch and be around. Critic Ben Brantley said it was worthy of a frontier *King Lear*, and he also pointed out how it allowed the park and its resident crazies to play a role in it. Subtlety and simplicity. The following is a hackneyed saying, and it is the one most dear to my heart when working with actors: The only stupid question is the one you don't ask. Be so thankful that the actors ask questions. You could never know what they need in order to fill the whole of the work that they have to do. A less experienced actor might have more to learn—and more energy to learn it with.

Listen to the audience. Smile. Once, I called a man to answer a question that he left on the Gorilla Rep phone line. What the question was, I don't remember. Maybe it was the lawn-chair question; I get that a lot. Whatever it was, I took the time to talk to him—not long, but enough to make sure he was comfortable and didn't have any more questions. Before we hung up, though, he asked me who I was. I told him my name. He said that was nice, but he had meant what was my job with the company. I told him that I had directed the show and, for what it was worth, that I was the founding artistic and producing director of it. If he wasn't happy with the show, the buck stopped with me. Again, he corrected me. "It's your company? And you called to answer my questions yourself? You'll go far!" Well, I've gotten further than I ever imagined I would, so I guess he was right, and there is something in it.

I am writing this book while sitting on a lawn, behind a bush, near a Sunday performance of *St. Mary's Catholic Girls School English 201 Class Presents Romeo and Juliet*. The assistant director and tech director have it under control, and they know how to summon me in an instant (call "cut!" loudly, of course). After a hard week, and a lot of setbacks and work, I can hear the audience laughing, and their attention is palpable. There is a cool breeze after a hot day. The sky is pink and purple, the streetlights provide an ambient light as the flood footlights set off the fountain behind the action, and the players look like figures in a Degas painting. The juice in my laptop is tapped from a streetlight. This is a good feeling, though not a crazy and ecstatic one. In a way, I am sitting on your set of your gorilla-theatre production. Under this sky, you work too. These stars can be a part of your set. It's beautiful!

All good things come from the work.

bibliography

An Acrobat of the Heart
By Stephen Wangh
Vintage Original 2000

Acting: The First Six Lessons
By Richard Boleslavsky
Theatre Arts Books 1933

Directing the Action: Acting and Directing in the Contemporary Theatre
By Charles Marowitz
Applause Theatre Book Publishers 1990

The Empty Space
By Peter Brook
Touchstone, Simon & Schuster 1968

Environmental Theater
By Richard Schechner
Applause Theatre Book Publishers 1993

Mr. William Shakespeare Comedies, Histories, and Tragedies: A Facsimile of the First Folio, 1623
Routledge 1998

Plays and Playwrights 2001: An Anthology
Edited by Martin Denton
The New York Theatre Experience 2001

Plays and Playwrights 2002: An Anthology
Edited by Martin Denton
New York Theatre Experience 2002

Plays and Playwrights 2003: An Anthology
Edited by Martin Denton
New York Theatre Experience 2003

Poetry, Language, Thought
by Martin Heidegger, translated by Albert Hofstadter
HarperCollins 1971

The Portable Jung
Edited with an introduction by Joseph Campbell
The Viking Press 1971

Science and Human Behavior
By B. F. Skinner
Free Press 1953

The Theater and Its Double
By Antonin Artaud, translated by Mary C. Richards
Grove/Atlantic 1972

Towards a Poor Theater
By Jerzy Grotowski
Routledge 2002

index